ADVANCED
SPEAKER DESIGNS
For the Hobbyist and Technician

ADVANCED
SPEAKER DESIGNS
For the Hobbyist and Technician

by Ray Alden

Contributing Technical Editor
Joseph A. D'Appolito, PhD
Audio and Loudspeaker Design Consultant

PROMPT.
PUBLICATIONS

An Imprint of
Howard W. Sams & Company
Indianapolis, Indiana

PROMPT® Publications is an imprint of Howard W. Sams & Company, 2647 Waterfront Parkway, East Drive, Suite 300, Indianapolis, IN 46214-2041

This book was originally developed and published as *Advanced Speaker Systems* by Master Publishing, Inc., 14 Canyon Creek Village MS 31, Richardson, Texas 75080.

International Standard Book Number: 0-7906-1070-1

Cover Design by: Suzanne Lincoln

Trademarks & Acknowledgments:
PC monitor displays have been identified as such for the particular software used.
TOP BOX is from TOP BOX, copyrighted © 1991 by J. D'Appolito
PXO is from PXO Passive Crossover CAD, copyrighted © 1992 by Robert M. Bullock III.
- Mylar and Kevlar are registered trademarks of E.I. DuPont DeNemours Co., Inc.
- IBM is a trademark of International Business Machines, Inc.
- MS-DOS and Microsoft are registered trademarks and Windows is a trademark of Microsoft Corporation.
- Apple and Macintosh are registered trademarks of Apple Computer, Inc.
- MLSSA is a trademark of DRA Laboratories.
- Focal is a registered trademark of Focal S.A.
- Formica is a registered trademark of Formica Corporation.
- Audax is a registered trademark of Audax Industries.
- Norsorex is a registered trademark of CDF Shimie.

All terms mentioned in this book that are known or suspected to be trademarks or services have been appropriately capitalized. PROMPT® Publications and Howard W. Sams & Company cannot attest to the accuracy of this information. Use of a term in this book should not be regarded as affecting the validity of any trademark or service mark.

Printed in the United States of America

9 8 7 6 5 4 3 2

Table of Contents

NOTE: The author used Radio Shack drivers (Table 4-2 and Table 4-3, pg. 40) when developing this book. Substitution of other drivers that do not have the exact same specifications or measured parameters will produce differing resultant data.

Preface

Advanced Speaker Designs is an outgrowth of a course I taught in speaker building at Stuyvesant High School in New York City. After teaching mathematics for 27 years, the often repeated student statement; "when will I ever use this" began to ring in my ears. It was apparent that there was a virtual absence of any course which applied mathematical abstractions. Many students felt that the only purpose of learning these abstraction was to regurgitate them on the feared math exams. In 1982, with support from the mathematics and industrial arts chairmen, I began a one term course in speaker building. In the first half, the theory was taught and the speakers were designed using mathematics. In the second half, the crossovers and the enclosures were built and the speakers assembled. The students clearly saw that mathematical knowledge could be combined with manual skills to make something they valued. Even other teachers took the course, which continues to this day. Before taking the speakers home, students brought in recorded music. As they listened to the music on their speakers, pride and joy were evident on their faces.

In writing *Advanced Speaker Designs*, I hope to bring the same pride and joy to you every time you play your completed speaker system. Even if you are a novice, with fading memories of high school math, *Advanced Speaker Designs* will help you to become a speaker designer. You may elect to build a speaker system first, by selecting one from Chapter 8, and return later to learn how to build your own unique system. By following instructions using easily available scientific calculators, you will be able to make quick work of complex equations. If you prefer to work on a personal computer, this book also gives tutorials on PC software that both eliminates the need to solve equations and quickly gives many design alternatives. At the same time, the book will give you an intuitive feeling for how speakers work.

The author would like to particularly thank Dr. Joseph D'Appolito for the generous contribution of his time in many discussions regarding topics in this book. Dr. D'Appolito is one of those rare people who simultaneously advances the state of the art and educates the public through his many articles and letters. Considerable thanks are due Diane Alden for the numerous hours in which she helped clarify and edit the original text. Thanks to Elliot Zalayet for many woodworking tips. Thanks also to many current and past colleagues at Stuyvesant High School: Michael D'Alleva, for both taming my unruly computers and taking over the course; Ed Marcantonio, Steve Kramer, Bob Rodney, Sandy Newman, Richard Rothberg and Al Tarendash for support in starting and maintaining the speaker-building course.

Ray Alden, January 1995

The Three Basic Components of Speaker Design

1

INTRODUCTION

There is a certain sense of pride and accomplishment when one is able to design and build speaker enclosures to include in an audio/visual system. As a result, the PROMPT Publications book, *Speakers for Your Home and Automobile*, was published to provide an easy-to-understand introduction to speaker enclosures, component specification, and design equations to build affordable, quality systems.

Advanced Speaker Systems takes the next step. It further clarifies the specifications of speaker drivers---even how to measure the parameters---and provides a means to deal with the more complicated mathematics needed to design more precise systems over a wide range of applications. There are three different approaches offered in this book:

1. If equations or computers seem too intimidating, go to Chapter 8 first. It contains complete speaker system plans. Select one and build your first system. The pride you will feel in a completed speaker system may give you the desire to return to the book and learn more so that the next system will be one of your own design.

2. If you don't have access to a computer, you can use a scientific calculator along with the information in this book to solve the equations needed to custom design your own speaker system. Chapters 3 and 4 show you how to manipulate the numbers in detail, so the mathematics will become manageable as you are guided through each step. This method takes a little more time, but the final results will be close or identical to those arrived at by using the computer program described in Chapter 5. Equations to find the component values used in crossovers are given in Chapter 7.

3. If you own a computer (or have access to one), this book will show you how to use a reasonably priced software program to perform the design operations, and will suggest more sophisticated software that can be used to calculate crossover networks. Computer programs provide an immediate picture of the projected results so that you can spend your time doing "what-if" scenarios instead of doing manual calculations. Most programs are available for computers running under MS-DOS® and some are available for the Apple® Macintosh®. Those of you who have Microsoft® Windows™ 3.1 can use the scientific calculator built into the Windows "Accessories" program group to verify the scientific calculator design calculations.

If you don't want to construct your own speaker enclosures, sources for both custom-built and ready-made enclosures of fixed volume are provided in the Appendix of this book. If you do want to build your own enclosures, but the woodworking presents a problem for you, the PROMPT Publications book, *Speakers for Your Home and Automobile*, provides some techniques and suggestions.

AN OVERALL SPEAKER SYSTEM

Let's begin our discussion by showing how a typical speaker system can be represented in three ways.

1. *Figure 1-1* shows the *block diagram* of a 2-way (two-driver) speaker system which consists of a crossover circuit, two speaker drivers, and an enclosure.
2. *Figure 1-2* shows the assembled speaker system in a *pictorial view* which is drawn so that you can see how the components are placed inside the enclosure.
3. *Figure 1-3* shows the *schematic diagram* of the speaker system. It shows the detailed electrical interconnections of the circuit components using standard schematic symbols.

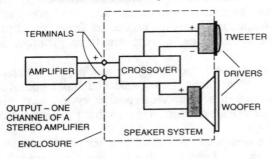

Figure 1-1. Block Diagram of 2-Way Speaker System

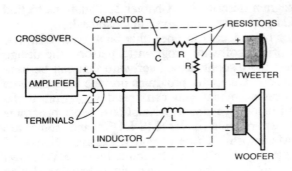

Figure 1-3. Schematic Diagram of 2-Way Speaker System

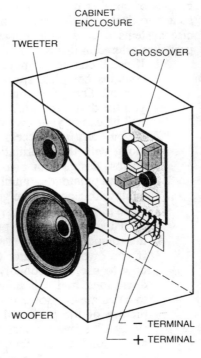

Figure 1-2. Exploded Pictorial View of 2-Way Speaker System

OVERVIEW OF THE SYSTEM

A system is called 2-way when two drivers are used. The drivers (commonly called speakers) contain the cones which actually move the air to convert electrical input signals into sound outputs. In a colorful reference to animals, the driver that reproduces the high-frequency sounds is called the tweeter, while the driver reproducing the low-frequency sounds is called the woofer. The enclosure, an important part of the design, has the prime function of extending the low frequencies so that the woofer will provide rich bass. Terminals, usually on the back of an enclosure, accept the wires coming from the amplifier output. Normally hidden from view inside the enclosure is the crossover, a passive electronic filter circuit consisting of capacitors, inductors and resistors. The wires from the terminals go directly to the crossover circuit and additional wires connect from the crossover to the drivers. In this 2-way system, the crossover, commonly called a crossover network, performs the very important task of dividing (filtering) the original broadband frequency signal from the amplifier into frequencies the respective drivers are designed to reproduce — high frequencies for the tweeter and low frequencies for the woofer.

The Driver

The driver is a complex device consisting of several important systems. Driver designers must pay close attention to these systems in order for the driver to perform well. As *Figure 1-4* shows, the driver consists of a frame housing the cone and voice coil (the moving system), the surround and the spider (the suspension system), and a permanent magnet system. The cone is connected to a cylinder (the former) around which a coil of enameled wire (voice coil) is wrapped. The signal coming from the amplifier/crossover passes through the voice coil, which is an inductor. It is called the voice coil because it causes the cone to move the air in front of the driver, thus giving the driver a voice. The voice coil is centered in a narrow gap through which the permanent magnet's field passes. One task of the surround, which suspends the cone on the basket, and the spider, which looks like a web, is to keep the voice coil centered in this narrow gap. Playing a speaker at such a loudness that it goes beyond its designed travel will very likely damage this critical alignment.

The cone moves because of a dynamic interaction between two magnetic fields, one coming from the permanent magnet and the other created by the signal voltage applied to the voice coil. *Figure 1-5a* shows that not only is a magnetic field created around an inductor when AC current flows, but that it also expands and collapses and changes direction each half cycle of the AC current's wave. The permanent magnet's field does not change direction. It remains highly concentrated and constant in the narrow gap between voice coil and magnet. When an incoming signal produces a voice-coil magnetic field that adds to and subtracts from the stationary field as shown in *Figure 1-5b,* the voice coil and the attached cone move forward. When the voice-coil signal's polarity reverses, the voice-coil field reverses, and the voice coil and cone move backward. Thus, the voice coil and the attached cone move forward and backward in accordance with the varying polarity of the signal applied to the voice coil. As the voice coil moves in the field of the permanent magnet, a voltage is induced in the voice coil to oppose the voltage applied to the voice coil. This is called the "counter-EMF" as shown in *Figure 1-5c*. Since counter-EMF opposes the original signal, it holds back or "damps" the voice-coil movement.

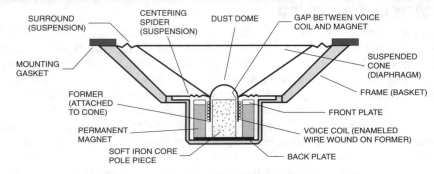

SURROUND (SUSPENSION)
CENTERING SPIDER (SUSPENSION)
DUST DOME
GAP BETWEEN VOICE COIL AND MAGNET
MOUNTING GASKET
SUSPENDED CONE (DIAPHRAGM)
FRAME (BASKET)
FORMER (ATTACHED TO CONE)
FRONT PLATE
PERMANENT MAGNET
VOICE COIL (ENAMELED WIRE WOUND ON FORMER)
SOFT IRON CORE POLE PIECE
BACK PLATE

Figure 1-4. A Paper or Polypropylene Cone Driver

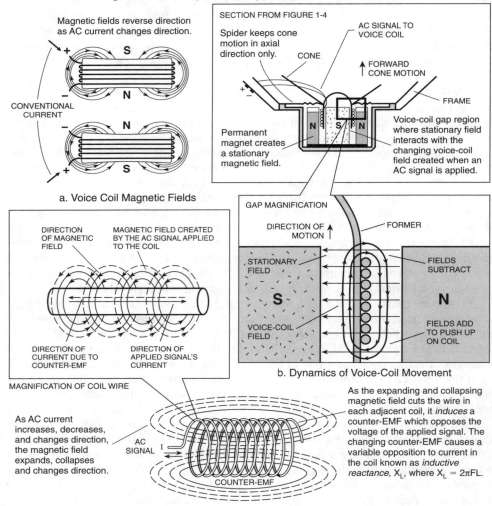

Magnetic fields reverse direction as AC current changes direction.

CONVENTIONAL CURRENT

a. Voice Coil Magnetic Fields

SECTION FROM FIGURE 1-4

AC SIGNAL TO VOICE COIL

Spider keeps cone motion in axial direction only.

CONE

FORWARD CONE MOTION

FRAME

Permanent magnet creates a stationary magnetic field.

Voice-coil gap region where stationary field interacts with the changing voice-coil field created when an AC signal is applied.

GAP MAGNIFICATION

DIRECTION OF MOTION

FORMER

DIRECTION OF MAGNETIC FIELD

MAGNETIC FIELD CREATED BY THE AC SIGNAL APPLIED TO THE COIL

STATIONARY FIELD

FIELDS SUBTRACT

S

N

VOICE-COIL FIELD

FIELDS ADD TO PUSH UP ON COIL

DIRECTION OF CURRENT DUE TO COUNTER-EMF

DIRECTION OF APPLIED SIGNAL'S CURRENT

b. Dynamics of Voice-Coil Movement

MAGNIFICATION OF COIL WIRE

As AC current increases, decreases, and changes direction, the magnetic field expands, collapses and changes direction.

AC SIGNAL

COUNTER-EMF

As the expanding and collapsing magnetic field cuts the wire in each adjacent coil, it *induces* a counter-EMF which opposes the voltage of the applied signal. The changing counter-EMF causes a variable opposition to current in the coil known as *inductive reactance*, X_L, where $X_L = 2\pi FL$.

c. Inductive Reactance of Coil (Inductor) Due to Counter-EMF

Figure 1-5. Inductor Magnetic Fields and Inductive Reactance

Cone Materials

Music is made up of sudden changes---the whack of a drum or pluck of a string--- sounds that are here and then gone very quickly. Such sounds are known as transients. A cone (or diaphragm) must be able to react quickly to reproduce such music transients accurately. Early in the development of drivers, heavy paper cones required strong permanent magnets to provide the strength for quick changes. Magnetic alloys for strong magnets were quite popular. Today, research concentrates on cone materials with a high *Young's Modulus*---a high stiffness-to-mass ratio---so it behaves like a rigid piston and yet is light. The cone needs to be able to change direction quickly with an appropriately sized magnet, not necessarily a super-strength magnet. Such cone materials range from commonly used polypropylene, to woven polykevlar, or "high-definition aerogel." Polykevlar is a sandwich of Kevlar® fibers and a compound of resin mixed with silica microspheres. High-definition aerogel is a composite matrix of acrylic polymer gel in which carbon and Kevlar fibers are imbedded.

THE ENCLOSURE
Reason for an Enclosure

If you have ever listened to a driver in free air---meaning "not in an enclosure"--- you may remember how thin it sounded. When that same driver is mounted in an enclosure, it produces a fuller sound. The free-air condition is known as an *acoustic short circuit*. *Figure 1-6* illustrates the front and rear low-frequency waves, which are 180° out of phase. As the cone moves forward, it compresses the air in front of it. At the same time, a region of low pressure is created behind the cone. If these two waves of pressure meet, they cancel each other. An enclosure prevents the two waves from meeting, thus extending the low-frequency response of a driver as compared to its performance in free air.

The Overall Enclosure

An enclosure design includes three important consideration: the shape of the enclosure, the material used to construct it, and the bracing used to prevent vibration of the enclosure. Constructing an enclosure requires the exact opposite strategy a luthier uses (a luthier builds stringed instruments). A guitar or violin relies on the harmonic overtones (integral multiples of a fundamental frequency) created by the wood to give the instrument a characteristic brilliance or richness. However, a speaker builder wants the speaker system to reproduce only the music from the original source, and not to alter the sound by its own panel resonances.

The Materials

Even a medium-sized enclosure panel can produce audible resonances in the woofer's range. These resonances can be altered by using braces on the panels. *Figure 1-7* shows that, as different braces break a 12" by 18" panel into smaller independent panels, higher pitched resonances are created.[1] The strategy shown in *Figure 1-7e* is especially effective for raising a panel's resonant frequency above the woofer's operating range. Three braces are placed parallel to the panel's long edge and are spaced unequally so that the resonance of each partition is different.

[1] Peter Muxlow, *Loudspeaker Cabinets,* Speaker Builder, Vol. 2, 1988

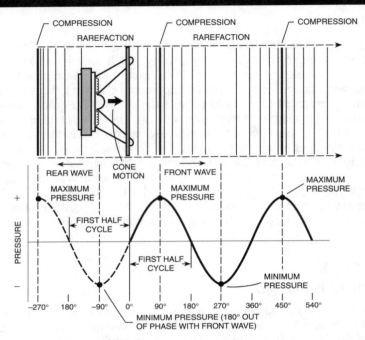

Figure 1-6. Analysis of the Front and Rear Wave of a Driver in Free Space

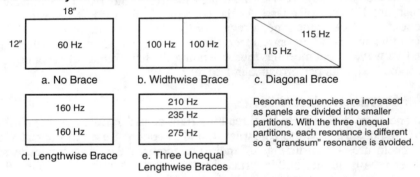

Resonant frequencies are increased as panels are divided into smaller partitions. With the three unequal partitions, each resonance is different so a "grandsum" resonance is avoided.

Figure 1-7. Cabinet Panel Resonance

Some materials are naturally more resonant than others; solid wood is perhaps the worst offender. Fiberboard is a good material for a speaker enclosure. It does not have a grain running in one direction so it does not have the large resonant tendencies of solid wood. A plastic laminate or real-wood veneer can be applied on the outside to make it attractive. Fiberboard comes in three densities: low, medium, and high. A premium medium-density fiberboard (MDF) is a good choice and will have less than 8% variation in density. MDF is available in 1/2″, 5/8″, 3/4″ and 1″ thicknesses. Two 3/4″ thick panels can be glued together with an ordinary panel adhesive to get a 1½″ thickness. Using a rubberized adhesive, such as silicone caulk, between panels instead of ordinary panel adhesive will further dampen panel vibrations. The use of thicker panels, adequate bracing, and a damping agent will go a long way toward providing sound with minimum enclosure coloration.

The Dimensions

Enclosure dimensions which determine an enclosure's shape are also an important issue for the quality of sound. In terms of waves created either inside or outside the enclosure, the worse case scenario is to use a cube shape. This shape can create intense standing waves inside the enclosure because of the symmetry of the shape. The listening room should also be included in this discussion, since it is the enclosure in which you hear the speaker's front wave. Waves are reflected along the axis (the width, height, and length) of an enclosure. A resonant frequency (one frequency "amplified" more than any other) is created when the speed of sound (1130 ft/s) is divided by twice the distance between the surfaces. For example, if an enclosure is built with L = 5', W = 5', and H = 5', then along each axis, the resonant frequency would be $1130/2 \times 5 = 113$ Hz. In addition, even more resonances are formed by integral multiples of the resonant frequency. In this example, each panel has the same second, third, fourth, etc. harmonics, which leads to a huge "pileup," or amplification, of resonance frequencies. To avoid this situation, the rectangular speaker enclosures should use either esthetic proportions such as those produced by the golden ratio $1.618 : 1 : 0.618$, or an acoustic ratio such as $0.7937 : 1 : 1.2599$. *Figure 1-8* shows how to calculate the external enclosure dimensions when the box's external volume is 1 cubic foot (1 ft^3). For different volumes, multiply the cubic feet by 1728 in order to get final results in inches and then follow the steps in *Figure 1-8*.

Enclosure Placement

While you can decide the dimensions of your enclosure prior to building, you are usually stuck with the dimensions of your room. In this regard, you are encouraged to experiment with speaker placement. One place to start in this war with room acoustics might be to take the length and width of your room and divide each by 3, 5, 7 and 9. It has been suggested that the intersection of lines connecting these points of division from opposite sides of the room pinpoint locations least likely to excite standing waves. Placement of a speaker in the corner of a room is considered the place most likely to set off standing waves.

How do you shape a cabinet for esthetic appeal and not create many common axial resonances?

Use the proportion 1.618 : 1 : 0.618. Given a 1 cubic foot external volume, give dimensions in inches of this enclosure. (1 cubic foot = 1728 cubic inches)

Using a scientific calculator:

STEP	PRESS	DISPLAY	DIMENSION
1.	1728		
2.	INV	1728	
3.	CUBE ROOT	12	WIDTH
4.	×	12	
5.	1.618	1.618	
6.	=	19.416	HEIGHT
7.	CLEAR		
8.	12	12	
9.	×	12	
10.	.618	.618	
11.	=	7.416	DEPTH

The dimensions H : W : D are: 19.4" : 12" : 7.42"

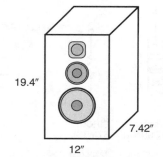

Similarly, dimensions can be obtained using the following acoustic ratio: 0.7937 : 1 : 1.2599

Figure 1-8. Shape of Enclosure

THE CROSSOVER

We will cover the crossover and the components used in its circuit in detail in Chapter 7; therefore, we will only deal here with some basic understanding of the circuit components: resistors, capacitors, and inductors. *Figure 1-9* shows the standard schematic symbols for a resistor, capacitor, and inductor as used in electrical circuits.

RESISTORS

A resistor is an electrical device which inhibits or opposes current (the flow of electrons) in an electrical circuit. A resistor is said to have one ohm of resistance when an electromotive force of one volt is needed to supply the energy to cause one ampere of current (6.25×10^{18} electrons per second) in a circuit. This relationship of voltage (E), current (I), and resistance (R) is called Ohm's law, which is expressed as $E = IR$. The unit of E is volts, of I is amperes, and of R is ohms. We can solve for R by rearranging the equation to $R = E/I$.

The main function of resistors in crossovers is attenuation. This function can be used to soften a driver that is too loud compared to other drivers in the speaker system. An sample circuit is shown in *Figure 1-3*. Typical resistor values used in a crossover range from 1 ohm to under 100 ohms. These resistors, usually of the ceramic type, must be able to handle from 5 watts to 25 watts of power. The power dissipated in a resistor is released in the form of heat.

Series and Parallel Circuits

Many times in designing crossover circuits, impedance compensation circuits, or attenuation circuits, you will not be able to obtain the exact value of resistors needed for the design. In that case, you will need to combine resistors in series or in parallel or both to obtain the right value. The equivalent resistance value, R_T, of resistors in *series*, as shown in *Figure 1-10a,* is the sum of all the resistance values in the series circuit. The equation is given in the figure. The equivalent resistance value, R_T, of resistors in *parallel*, as shown in *Figure 1-10b,* is always less than the smallest resistance value in the parallel circuit. Various equations used to calculate the equivalent resistance are given in the figure.

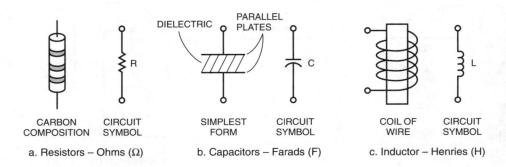

a. Resistors – Ohms (Ω)   b. Capacitors – Farads (F)   c. Inductor – Henries (H)

Figure 1-9. Identifying Resistors, Capacitors, and Inductors

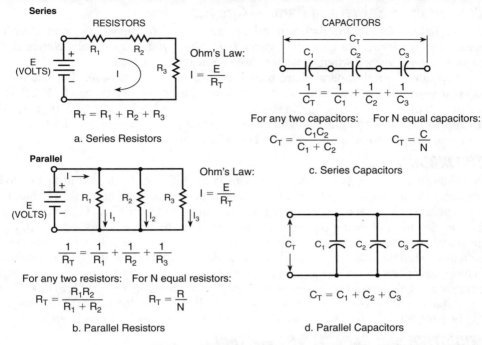

Figure 1-10. Resistors and Capacitors in Series and Parallel

In Chapter 8, you are sometimes asked to use resistors with odd values such as 5.7 ohms. Purchasing such a resistor is often impossible. You are usually able to find values such as 4 ohms, 8 ohms, 10 ohms or 20 ohms. Using the formula for two unequal resistors in parallel, shown in *Figure 1-10b*, you can often form odd values. For example, if you wire a 20-ohm resistor in parallel with a 8-ohm resistor, you will have one equivalent resistor with a total resistance of 5.7 ohms.

THE CAPACITOR

A capacitor is an electrical device which stores an electrical charge. As shown in *Figure 1-9b*, a capacitor, in its simplest form, can be made from two parallel plates separated by a dielectric (insulator). In an AC circuit, capacitors provide an opposition to current known as capacitive reactance, X_C. In Chapter 7, we will show that one of the main functions of a capacitor used in a crossover is to prevent a majority of low frequencies from reaching the tweeter.

The basic unit of capacitance is the farad (F). One farad represents the ability of a capacitor to store one coulomb of charge (6.25×10^{18} electrons) when an electromotive force of one volt is applied across the plates. Electronic circuits, including crossovers, commonly use capacitance values measured in microfarads (μF), which is one millionth of a farad. To convert farads to microfarads, multiply by one million (10^6). For example, to convert 0.0000137 F into microfarads, multiply 0.0000137 F by 10^6. This amounts to moving the decimal point six places to the right, giving 13.7 μF.

Capacitors may be polarized or non-polarized (nonpolar). Nonpolar capacitors are always used in a crossover so that it operates properly and reliably in the circuit.

Capacitors in Series and Parallel Circuits

The equations for determining equivalent capacitance of capacitors connected in series and in parallel are given in *Figures 1-10c* and *1-10d,* respectively. Notice that capacitance values add when capacitors are connected in parallel.

Capacitors wired in parallel are useful when building a crossover. For example, say you need a 13.7 µF capacitor for the crossover, but the store only has 1 µF, 2.2 µF, 3.7 µF, 4.9 µF, 6.8 µF and 8.8 µF in stock. By choosing a 1 µF, 2.2 µF, 3.7 µF, and 6.8 µF and wiring all of them in parallel, you have what you need: an equivalent 13.7 µF capacitor. Or you could use a 4.9 µF and an 8.8 µF wired in parallel.

THE INDUCTOR

We showed in *Figure 1-5* that a coil of wire is an inductor, how current in the coil produces the inductive effect, and that the opposition to AC current is called inductive reactance, X_L. In Chapter 7, we will show the main function of X_L is to keep high frequencies from reaching the woofer. The unit for inductance is the henry (H), but most crossover inductors have values in millihenries ($\frac{1}{1000}$ of a henry). Crossover inductors often must be custom made because the required odd values are not stocked in electronic parts stores. Equivalent inductance values in series and parallel inductive circuits are calculated the same as for resistance values in resistive circuits. The equations in *Figure 1-10a* for series resistors and in *Figure 1-10b* for parallel resistors can be used for inductors by substituting L for R in every position in each equation.

INDUCTIVE AND CAPACITIVE REACTANCE

Both inductors and capacitors have a variable opposition to current (like resistance) in an AC circuit that depends on the frequency of the circuit voltage source. This opposition is called *reactance* because of the unique reaction to each frequency. The equations for inductive reactance, X_L, and capacitive reactance, X_C, are as follows:

$$X_L = 2\pi FL$$

$$X_C = \frac{1}{2\pi FC}$$

Where:
F = frequency in **hertz (Hz)**
L = inductor in **henries (H)**
π = 3.14159

C = capacitor in **farads (F)**
X_C = capacitive reactance in **ohms**
X_L = inductive reactance in **ohms**

The change in reactance as a 0.001 henry (1 mH) inductor and a 0.0001 farad (100 µF) capacitor are subjected to frequencies of 10 Hz, 500 Hz, 1000 Hz, 5000 Hz and 15,000 Hz are as follows

Frequency	10 Hz	500 Hz	1000 Hz	5000 Hz	15,000 Hz
X_L when L = 0.001 henry	0.06 ohms	3.1 ohms	6.3 ohms	31 ohms	94 ohms
X_C when C = 0.0001 farad	159 ohms	3.2 ohms	1.6 ohms	0.32 ohms	0.1 ohms

Notice that as the frequencies increases, the inductive reactance increases. This happens, as shown in *Figure 1-5c,* because higher frequencies induce more counter-EMF in the adjacent inductor windings. With the capacitor, the reverse happens; that is, capacitive reactance decreases as frequency increases. These important results indicate that inductors and capacitors can be used to block certain frequencies from reaching either a woofer or a tweeter. This will be used to a great extent in Chapter 7, which deals with the crossover.

Driver Parameters – Their Meaning and Measurement

Each driver used in a speaker system is unique, not only in appearance, but in terms of how it will behave, both acoustically and electrically. Because all drivers with moving voice coils operate in a comparable manner, we use numbers called *parameters* to describe and specify the behavior of drivers, allowing us to distinguish one driver from another. Two engineers, Neville Thiele and Richard Small, did a great deal of work to show how these parameters define the interaction of a driver with an enclosure and, consequently, they have come to be called *Thiele-Small parameters*. Rather than blindly applying these numbers in formulas or computer programs, it would be wise for you to have an understanding of the meaning of each parameter. With this understanding, when you need a driver for a certain purpose, you will find that the parameters will guide you toward choosing the driver most appropriate for your needs. The Thiele-Small driver parameters we will use in this chapter are F_S, F_C, Q_{TS}, Q_{MS}, Q_{ES}, Q_{TC}, V_{AS}, C_{MS}, and S_D.

THE F_S PARAMETER

On July 1, 1940 the Tacoma Narrows, a suspension bridge located on Pudget Sound, Washington, opened to traffic. Four months later a mild gale, which produced a fluctuating wind force that matched the bridge's natural resonant frequency, set the main span oscillating with such great undulations that it ripped the section apart, finally collapsing the whole structure. After this event, considerations such as damping were designed into bridges to make them aerodynamically sound, avoiding future disasters.

When weights are suspended, such as in the bridge described above or as in a cone in the frame of a driver, the whole system will have a *resonant frequency*, F_S, in hertz (cycles per second) abbreviated Hz. At the resonant frequency, the *inertial effects* of a "dead" weight combine with an "energetic" suspension so that they balance each other. And, when excited, if it were not for friction, the system would oscillate in an endless recurring or *periodic motion*. With regards to a speaker, it is important for the resonant frequency of a driver to be properly controlled when the driver is placed in an enclosure. With an inferior design, the effects on the sound of a speaker system could be as disastrous as the wind was for the structure of the Tacoma Narrows bridge.

Sine-Wave Periodic Motion

The study of periodic motion was of particular importance in the 17th century to assist mariners, who needed an accurate clock to determine longitude while at sea.

The swinging of a pendulum was studied by Galileo Galilei, who used his own heartbeat to time the swinging of lamps suspended on long cords in cathedrals. Years later, Robert Hooke, a noted experimentalist and contemporary of Isaac Newton, began to ponder the up and down oscillations of a weight suspended on a spring as shown in *Figure 2-1a*. This system matches the construction of a driver as shown in *Figure 2-1b*, where a weight (the cone and voice coil) is suspended by a spring (the surround and the spider). If you pull down on the weight suspended on the spring shown in *Figure 2-1a*, upon release the weight will bob up and down at a uniform rate, which is the natural resonant frequency of the system.

Figure 2-2 illustrates how the motion of the weight in a spring and mass system produces the same pattern of sinusoidal waves as sound. Pushing and releasing a woofer's cone will not make it continually bob up and down because such motion is heavily damped by the suspension system; however, if you place your ear *close* and give the cone a "thump" with your finger, you may be able to discern a telltale sound giving an inkling of the resonant frequency. Deeper tones indicate lower resonant frequencies.

The amazing discovery that Hooke made was that, whether you pull down on the weight a little bit or a lot, *the time it takes for one complete oscillation (the period, T) is the same*. If you pull the weight down a great distance, it is true that the spring's restoring force will pull it up very fast, but the period will be the same if you pull it down only a short distance!

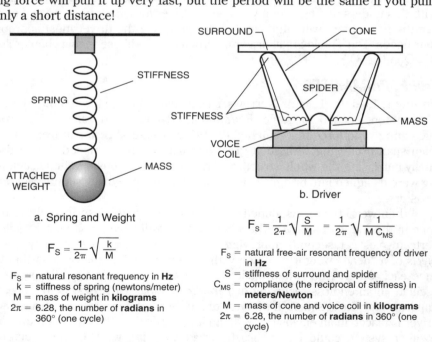

a. Spring and Weight

$$F_S = \frac{1}{2\pi}\sqrt{\frac{k}{M}}$$

F_S = natural resonant frequency in **Hz**
k = stiffness of spring (newtons/meter)
M = mass of weight in **kilograms**
2π = 6.28, the number of **radians** in 360° (one cycle)

b. Driver

$$F_S = \frac{1}{2\pi}\sqrt{\frac{S}{M}} = \frac{1}{2\pi}\sqrt{\frac{1}{M\,C_{MS}}}$$

F_S = natural free-air resonant frequency of driver in **Hz**
S = stiffness of surround and spider
C_{MS} = compliance (the reciprocal of stiffness) in **meters/Newton**
M = mass of cone and voice coil in **kilograms**
2π = 6.28, the number of **radians** in 360° (one cycle)

Figure 2-1. Spring/Mass System vs Driver Suspension/Cone System

Equations for F_S

Exactly what does affect the natural resonant frequency of the spring and mass system? There are really only two things you can fiddle with — *the strength of the*

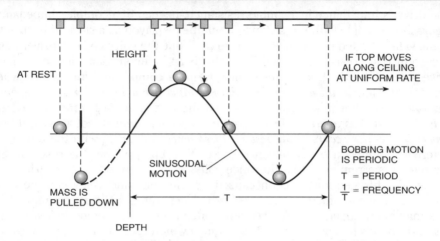

Figure 2-2. Periodic Motion of Spring and Mass System

spring used and the amount of mass attached. Robert Hooke described how spring strength and mass affect the natural resonant frequency, F_S, through the equation:

$$2\pi F_S = \sqrt{\frac{k}{M}}$$

In this equation, k represents the strength or the *stiffness of the spring* being used; k gets larger as the spring approaches the caliber of Arnold Schwarzenegger's muscle. What does it mean if the spring gets stiffer and, thus, k gets larger? Since $2\pi F_S$ gets larger as k gets larger, the only term in this product that can vary is frequency, F_S, since 2π ($2 \times 3.14 = 6.28$) is a constant. Therefore, *larger values of k result in higher resonant frequencies.* In the case of a driver, if driver designers use a suspension system in a driver that is *not compliant,* which is to say they use a *stiff* surround and spider, and all else remains the same, then the driver will have a *higher resonant frequency.* The M in the equation's denominator is the attached mass and, since $2\pi F$ is inversely proportional to the square root of M, it means that *larger masses produce smaller F_S values, resulting in lower frequencies.* One way for designers to get a driver with a low resonant frequency is to use a heavy cone (large M) and/or a more compliant (small k) suspension system. This explains why the relatively heavier cones of woofers give you drivers of low resonant frequency, whereas the comparatively lighter cones of tweeters produce much higher resonant frequencies.

Determining Driver F_S

As stated previously, F_S is the free-air resonant frequency for a driver. The equation for F_S of a driver was given in *Figure 2-1.* The important value of F_S is almost always given, along with the other Thiele-Small parameters, on the specification sheet that comes with a driver. If F_S is not given, then another technique must be used to determine F_S. You need to look at the *impedance curve* of the driver.

An example of an impedance curve is shown in *Figure 2-3.* When the driver impedance is given as 8 ohms or 4 ohms, you are led to the oversimplified conclusion that the driver's impedance is a simple resistance, instead of a complex impedance. On *Figure 2-3,* a simple 8-ohm resistance would be displayed as a straight horizontal line at the value of rated impedance, not a curve. While the voice coil of a driver has a direct-current (DC) resistance called R_E, it also is an inductor. Since inductors have inductive reactance, which, with resistance, forms a complicated impedance when subjected to AC signals, *the driver voice coil impedance is not a simple resistance, but a complex impedance.* For this reason, *Figure 2-3* shows that *the impedance of a typical driver is represented as a curve which varies as frequency changes,* not a straight line. *Maximum impedance occurs at the resonant frequency,* linking F_S with the top of the characteristic "bump" in the impedance curve. This bump within the resonant frequency region is a reminder that the voice coil acts as a generator of electricity. At resonance, F_S, this generator action caused by the cone and voice coil vibrating together is at a maximum (most energetic) and generates the most counter-EMF, giving a maximum impedance. As frequency increases in the region below F_S, the counter-EMF builds to maximum, and as frequency increases in the region above F_S, the counter-EMF decreases from maximum. The "valley" after that mountainous bump, before the curve starts to climb again, is the region which determines whether drivers are nominally called "8-ohm" or "4-ohm" drivers. This is the *region of rated impedance.* Later in this chapter, you will be shown a test routine that will enable you to find the impedance curve and F_S of a driver in *free air* (i.e., when a driver is not placed in a cabinet). When a driver is placed in a closed box, F_S rises to a higher value, called F_C. The reason for this will be explained in the next chapter.

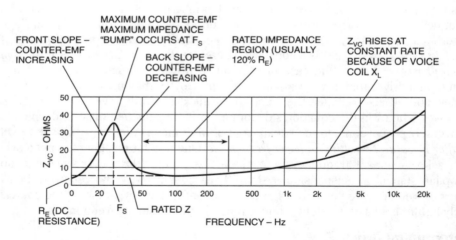

Figure 2-3. Impedance Curve of a Typical Driver

THE Q PARAMETER

Recall that the Tacoma Narrows bridge collapsed because there was hardly any control in the suspension system while winds whipped it into maximum motion at resonance. The driver parameter Q is a measure of the amount of control, coming from electrical and mechanical damping, that a driver has at resonance. Two drivers could have the same F_S and yet, because of different Q values, have very different behavior around resonance. For example, let us look at two nearly identical drivers with the same F_S, except the first driver has a hefty magnet while the second has a puny one. A strong magnet, interacting with the magnetic field from the driver's voice coil, will have a robust controlling effect on cone motion. The first driver, having the strong magnet, has the ability to rapidly "kick start" the cone at the outset of a musical transient or, conversely, it quickly brakes (dampens) the cone's movement after that transient has gone. The first driver is said to have a better *transient response* than the second one.

A second manifestation of this "control" can be found in how loud (measured in dB) a driver responds at resonance. The driver with the puny magnet will not exert much control on the substantial cone motion occurring at resonance. It will have a *louder* response at resonance than it would if it had the stronger magnet. When you design speaker systems, you must make a *compromise between transient response and how loud a driver responds at resonance*. In the next chapter, you will be introduced to equations which will enable you to design a closed box speaker system. With these equations, you will be able to balance the two aspects of Q to your liking. Q_{TS} describes the Q of a speaker in free air and, just as happens with F_S, it will change to a larger value, called Q_{TC}, when the driver is placed in a closed box.

Q_{TS}

Q_{TS} is composed of two elements, Q_{ES} and Q_{MS}, the electrical and mechanical Qs, respectively, of the driver. The Q_{MS} is the control coming from the suspension system's damping abilities. Entirely new surround materials, such as norsorex™, have been developed for this purpose. A ball of norsorex, which feels like rubber, has virtually no bounce when dropped. Rather than exerting a linear restoring force, norsorex disperses the energy from the fall in all directions. This and similar kinds of materials behave somewhat like a shock absorber, damping jolts and flexing in the cone. The Q_{ES} is a gauge of the control on a driver coming from the counter-EMF generated in the voice coil. Q_{ES} is usually a smaller value than Q_{MS}, meaning that the electrical damping is the primary controller of the driver's behavior near resonance. Q_{TS}, the total Q of the driver, is obtained by using a "product over sum" equation:

$$Q_{TS} = \frac{Q_{ES} \times Q_{MS}}{Q_{ES} + Q_{MS}}$$

Q_{TC}

Once a driver is enclosed, the Q_{TS} value changes to Q_{TC}. High values of Q_{TC} are called *underdamped* because they do not exert as much control over the driver response as do smaller values of Q_{TC}, which can so curtail driver response that they are known as *overdamped*. The ability of Q_{TC} to control response at resonance is illustrated in *Figure 2-4*. Looking at this figure you may say, "Wow! I'll take the big Q_{TC} of 2. I want a lot of bass for my money!" In terms of cost, this will probably be the case, since drivers with high Q_{TC} often have the less expensive small magnets. However, the real price you pay for this "bargain" is that the same lack of control which allowed the big response at resonance also furnishes poor control over transients, causing an affliction known as *ringing*. As shown in *Figure 2-4,* the higher the Q_{TC}, the greater the ringing in the transient response. Closed box speakers with a $Q_{TC} > 2$ (the bass of a

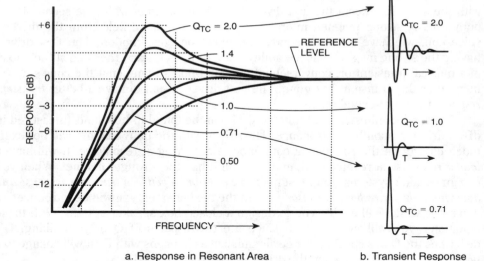

a. Response in Resonant Area   b. Transient Response

Figure 2-4. Two Characteristic Reponses of Speaker Systems with Various Q_{TC}

speaker with a Q_{TC} of 2 has a 6-dB increase above the reference level) will deliver an increasingly murky or thudding sound, particularly compared to those with a $Q_{TC} < 1$. Speaker enclosures with high Q_{TC} values can obscure the sharply focused details of music in the bass region. Many designers opt for a compromise in the final Q_{TC}, aiming for values nested between $0.7 < Q_{TC} < 1.1$. This allows for both a good transient response and a decent bass response.

The V_{AS} Parameter

Recall that in the spring and mass system, S is the stiffness of the spring, and that compliance C_{MS} is the reciprocal of stiffness, or $C_{MS} = 1/S$. In a driver system, C_{MS} is the compliance of the spider and surround suspension system. When the compliance of a driver (C_{MS}) is expressed in the meter-kilogram-second (MKS) system, it is expressed in meters (distance) per Newton (force). One meter/Newton means that it will take a force of one Newton to move an object (like a cone) one meter. However, C_{MS} is not expressed in its most useful form when you wish to calculate how a driver will match to a box of a specific volume.

In order to help with this computation, engineers have changed compliance into a form expressed as a volume of air called V_{AS}. When a volume of air is compressed as it is in a bicycle pump, it will exert a counter or restoring force. Air volume can be considered equivalent to compliance since, in order to compress an enclosed volume of air one meter, it will take a specific force measured in Newtons. The driver parameter, V_{AS}, called the *equivalent volume of compliance*, specifies a volume of air having the same compliance as the suspension system of the driver.

For example, *Figure 2-5* shows two boxes, each with a piston of the same size used to compress the air in the box. Each piston is pushed down the *same distance*.

Container #1 has a large volume; container #2 has a small volume. The force required to push the piston down the same distance in each container is much larger for container #2 than for container #1. *A large volume of air is more compliant than a small volume of air.* A small volume of air is quite stiff. Since a driver acts like the piston in *Figure 2-5*, then, using the effective piston area of a driver (S_D), a driver's compliance (C_{MS}) can be converted to V_{AS} using the following equation.

$$V_{AS} = 1.40 \times 10^5 \times C_{MS} \times S_D{}^2$$

where: 1.40×10^5 = a **constant** representing air density and the speed of sound.
V_{AS} = Volume in **cubic meters**
C_{MS} = Compliance in **meters/Newton**
S_D = Cone area of driver in **square meters**

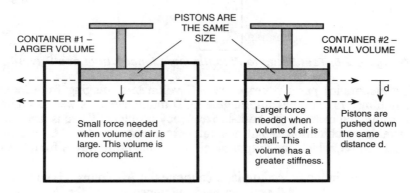

Figure 2-5. Compliance of a Volume of Air

The F_S, Q_{TS} and V_{AS} Thiele-Small driver parameters are the three absolute minimum values you need to design a closed or vented speaker enclosure. They are normally given on specification sheets regularly provided with drivers. However, variations in a batch of drivers can occur during different production runs, particularly in the compliance of the suspension systems, leading to different Q_{TS} values, and as much as a 50% change in V_{AS}. There is general accord that a 20% variation in V_{AS} will not have serious effect on the final system response. Nonetheless, many designers feel it valuable to measure these parameters. The more dedicated you are to excellent sound, the more you may wish to have your final designs based on the most accurate measured results. The next section will show you how to do this.

MEASURING DRIVER IMPEDANCE

The test setup for measuring driver impedance is shown in *Figure 2-6*. The equipment required is:

1. An AC voltmeter
2. An *audio frequency* sine-wave signal generator (not radio frequency)
3. A frequency counter
4. A 1000-ohm resistor (rated 1 to 5 watts)
5. A 10-ohm (high precision ± 1%) resistor
6. Some "hook-up" wire
7. The driver you want to measure

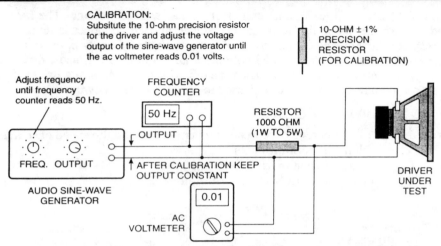

Figure 2-6. Test Setup to Find the Impedance Curve of a Driver

Most electronics parts stores carry AC voltmeters, ranging from inexpensive analog multimeters to digital autoranging LCD multimeters, as well as digital, true-RMS autoranging meters with built-in frequency counters. There is are also generally available combination signal generator-frequency counters. An example is a BK Model 3011B, which can output precisely counted sine waves from 0.2 Hz to 2 MHz.

The first step in the procedure is to calibrate the AC voltmeter, so that by multiplying the reading by 1000 you can read the impedance of the driver directly on the meter. Calibrate by inserting the 10-ohm resistor in place of the driver and adjusting the voltage output on the audio frequency sine-wave generator until the AC voltmeter reads 0.01 volt. With the voltmeter calibrated, keep that output voltage setting, take out the 10-ohm resistor and put the driver in the circuit. Now vary the frequency control on the audio frequency generator, but not the output, and you will see the voltage readings change. A reading of 0.005 volt represents 5 ohms, 0.01 volt represents 10 ohms, and 0.0156 volt represents 15.6 ohms. In other words, to convert the voltmeter reading directly into ohms, simply multiply the reading by 1000 (10^3) or move the decimal three places to the right. If you have an AC voltmeter that can read down to 1 Hz then, since 1 Hz is so close to 0 Hz, you may take this voltmeter reading as the DC resistance (R_E) of the driver. Otherwise, an independent measurement of R_E is necessary. Record the impedance readings at regular increments of frequency using smaller increments on each side of the maximum impedance (R_{MAX}). When you plot the readings, the impedance curve versus frequency should look similar to the one shown in *Figure 2-3*.

HOW TO FIND F_S, Q_{MS}, Q_{ES} AND Q_{TS}

Now that you have the impedance curve, you can determine the driver parameters F_S, Q_{MS}, Q_{ES} and Q_{TS}. To illustrate how, let's examine an unknown and inexpensive 6 1/2" polypropylene cone driver. The rear of this driver exposes a very small magnet. When the cone is thumped, it creates a tone that is not particularly deep. The puny looking magnet indicates that there would probably not be much control around resonance. From this, we can infer that the Q_{TS} of the driver is probably large and that F_S is likely high. Let us find the impedance curve and the Q_{TS} of this driver using the test setup of *Figure 2-6*, and compare our results to our simple "look and listen" experiment.

Play about 30 minutes of music through the driver to loosen the suspension system. Calibrate the test setup and insert the driver into the test setup. Start the frequency at 1 Hz, which gives R_E. Change the frequency in increments as indicated in *Figure 2-7*. For each frequency, read and record the impedance from the voltmeter. Slowly change the frequency around the maximum impedance reading, locating R_{MAX} and the resonant frequency, F_S. With R_E, F_S and R_{MAX}, you computer R_O, R_X, Q_{MS}, Q_{ES} and Q_{TS} using the following procedure. The equation are summarized in *Figure 2-7*. Remember to check V in *Figure 2-6* to make sure it stays constant at the calibration voltage as frequency changes.

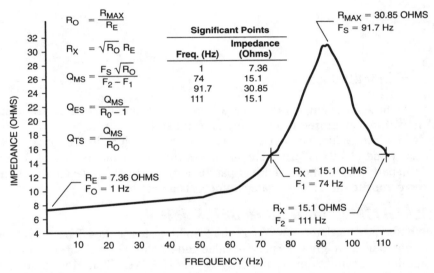

Figure 2-7. Determining F_S, Q_{MS}, Q_{ES} and Q_{TS} from the Impedance Curve

Procedure to Find F_S, Q_{MS}, Q_{ES} and Q_{TS}

1. One hertz is virtually the same as 0 Hz which is DC resistance, therefore, use
$R_E = 7.36$ ohms.
2. The maximum impedance is 30.85 ohms at 91.7 Hz; therefore,
$F_S = 91.7$ Hz
$R_{MAX} = 30.85$ ohms.
3. Now we can find R_O:
$R_O = R_{MAX}/R_E$
$R_O = 30.85/7.36$
$R_O = 4.19157$
4. From R_0 we can find a reference impedance called R_X.
$R_X = (\sqrt{R_0})(R_E)$
$R_X = (\sqrt{4.19157})(7.36)$

$$R_X = (2.0473)(7.36)$$
$$R_X = 15.068 \text{ ohms}$$

5. Observe the data to find two frequencies, one below F_S and one above F_S, whose impedances are equal to R_X (15.1 ohms). Call them F_1 and F_2. By observation, $F_1 = 74$ Hz and $F_2 = 111$ Hz.

Note: If F_1 and F_2 are accurate, then $F_S = \sqrt{(F_1 F_2)}\ \pm 1$ Hz. For example, substituting: $\sqrt{(74 \times 111)} = 90.63$ Hz, which is within 1.07 Hz of 91.7 Hz.

6. $Q_{MS} = F_S\ (\sqrt{R_0})/(F_2 - F_1)$
   $Q_{MS} = 91.7 \times (2.0473)/(111 - 74)$
   $Q_{MS} = 5.15$
7. $Q_{ES} = Q_{MS}/(R_0 - 1)$
   $Q_{ES} = 5.15/(4.19157 - 1)$
   $Q_{ES} = 1.61$
8. $Q_{TS} = (Q_{ES})(Q_{MS})/(Q_{ES} + Q_{MS})$
   $Q_{TS} = 1.2286$
   OR
   $Q_{TS} = Q_{MS}/R_0$
   $Q_{TS} = 5.15/4.19157$
   $Q_{TS} = 1.2286$

Thus, we find our example driver has a $F_S = 91.7$ Hz and $Q_{TS} = 1.23$. Compared to woofers with resonant frequencies ranging from 20 Hz to 50 Hz, we see that 91.7 Hz is indeed a high value. Similarly, compared with Q_{TS} values in the range $0.18 < Q_{TS} < 0.6$, a value of 1.23 is large. This indicates that the "look and listen" test can provide "ball-park" expectations of driver parameters. If we now move forward to find V_{AS}, we can complete the Thiele-Small parameter triumvirate.

THE "ADDED MASS" METHOD TO DETERMINE V_{AS}

Most methods used to determine V_{AS} require building test boxes. The one chosen here does not. It uses weights of a precise value added symmetrically around the dust cap to shift the resonant frequency down by at least 25%. We will use the same driver as we used in the previous example. The Department of the Mint of the United States Treasury provides us with an excellent source of precise nonmagnetic weights, namely the nickel coin, which is a consistent and exact 5 grams. If we place six nickels around the dust cap, then we have added 30 grams, or 0.03 kilogram (kg), to the weight of the cone. Remember, if you increase the mass of the cone, then the driver will have a lower resonant frequency. If we again test the impedance of the 6½" driver, we find the new resonant frequency, F'_S, is 43.7 Hz; it has been shifted down to 48% of F_S.

Determining C_{MS}

The compliance of the driver can be now calculated using the equation:

$$C_{MS} = [1/(2\pi)^2 \times M] \times [(F_S + F'_S) \times (F_S - F'_S)/(F_S \times F'_S)^2]$$

where:

   M = The *added* mass in **kilograms**
   C_{MS} = Compliance in **meters/Newton**

Substituting the values we know for M, F_S and F'_S, we obtain:

$$C_{MS} = [1/6.28^2 \times 0.03] \times [(91.7 + 43.7) \times (91.7 - 43.7)/(91.7 \times 43.7)^2]$$
$$C_{MS} = 0.3421 \times 10^{-3} \text{ meters/Newton}$$

Now we can convert C_{MS} to V_{AS} using the equation:

$$V_{AS} = 1.4 \times 10^5 \times S_D^2 \times C_{MS}$$

S_D is the "effective" piston area in square meters and V_{AS} is in cubic meters. We need to determine S_D.

Determining S_D and V_{AS}

S_D is a bit crankier than the title implies. The surround also acts as part of this effective piston area, leaving us with a slightly "fuzzy" variable having an effect on V_{AS}. Including half the surround on each side of the cone as part of the "effective" diameter helps to approximate the true piston area. This shows why V_{AS} is a more difficult parameter to measure precisely unless you are willing to build test boxes. Using our example 6½" driver, the "effective" piston diameter measures 13.3 cm. Since 100 cm = 1 meter, the radius (R) = (0.133/2) meter = 0.0665 meter. We can calculate the approximate "effective" piston area (A) using $A = \pi R^2$, thus, A = 0.0139 square meter. Substituting S_D = 0.0139 m² and C_{MS} = 0.3421 m/N into the V_{AS} equation, we find:

$$V_{AS} = 1.4 \times 10^5 \times 0.0139^2 \times 0.3421 \times 10^{-3}$$

Recall that the laws of exponents tell us $(10^5)(10^{-3}) = 10^{5-3} = 10^2$. Substituting, we find:

$$V_{AS} = 1.4 \times 0.000193 \times 0.3421 \times 10^2 = 0.00924 \text{ cubic meter}$$

Since 1 cubic meter = 35.314 cubic feet, then multiplying 0.00924 by 35.314 gives:

$$V_{AS} = 0.326 \text{ cubic feet.}$$

To summarize, we have found the parameters of this 6½" driver to be

$$F_S = 91.7 \text{ Hz}, Q_{TS} = 1.23, \text{ and } V_{AS} = 0.326 \text{ ft}^3$$

If you put this driver in a closed box, F_S and Q_{TS} will become even higher! In the next chapter, we will use the parameters we measured for this driver in the equations used to design a closed box in order to see what will result. It may well be that this driver would work better as a midrange in a 3-way system, or perhaps as the woofer in a small surround-sound system where economy is more important than deep bass.

THE VOICE COIL INDUCTANCE

We have learned that the voice coil is an inductor. It is worth knowing the amount of inductance in millihenries (mH), especially since this information will be asked by the software that will be used later in this book. Unfortunately, this information is not always given in the specification sheet of a driver. The way to find it is to use the impedance curve of a driver, particularly as the frequencies become large. Impedance varies with frequency and depends on the inductive and capacitive characteristics of the driver as well as its DC resistance. As frequencies get higher, capacitive effects diminish and the rise in impedance over DC resistance, as shown in *Figure 2-3*, is attributed mainly to voice coil inductance. Manufacturers typically measure voice coil inductance at or near 1000 Hz (1 kHz).

Method to Determine the Voice Coil Inductance

Using the test setup as before, and using the frequencies given in *Figure 2-8,* we find the impedance values for the 6½″ driver as shown in *Figure 2-8.* Recall that we found the DC resistance of the voice coil to be 7.36 ohms. When we look at a high frequency such as 1421 Hz, we find the impedance has increased to 9.51 ohms. We can attribute this increase to the voice coil reactance. At first look, the voice coil reactance would seem to be 9.51 ohms − 7.36 ohms = 2.51 ohms. From *Figure 2-8,* we see that inductive reactance and resistance do not obey the simple arithmetic of resistors. We must use the mathematics of the right triangle to add vectors which are 90° out of phase. The voice coil reactance X_L and the resistance R_E are 90° out of phase so we must use the Pythagorean theorem:

$$Z^2 = R_E{}^2 + X_L{}^2$$

At 1421 Hz, Z = 9.51 ohms, R_E = 7.36 ohms and X_L is unknown.

Solving for X_L:

$$X_L{}^2 = Z^2 - R_E{}^2$$
$$X_L = \sqrt{Z^2 - R_E{}^2}$$

Substituting:

$$X_L = \sqrt{9.51^2 - 7.36^2}$$
$$X_L = 6.022 \text{ ohms}$$

Recall the formula for inductive reactance:

$$X_L = 2\pi FL$$

Solving for L:

$$L = \frac{X_L}{2\pi F}$$

Substituting:

$$L = \frac{6.022}{6.28 \times 1421}$$

$$L = 0.0006748 \text{ henries or } 0.67 \text{ mH}$$

HOW TO MEASURE THE FREQUENCY RESPONSE OF A DRIVER

In order to know whether two drivers can be used together in a 2-way speaker system, you must determine if the frequency response of the woofer and the tweeter overlap. A crossover cannot "add" a missing section of frequency response to the natural frequency response of either driver; it can only filter off a section. If a frequency response is not supplied with the driver, the only way to find this response is to measure it. If you attempt to use an audio oscillator to apply frequencies from 20 Hz to 20 kHz to the driver in an ordinary room, it will lead to room reverberations that will wreak havoc with the measurements. Not long ago, the only way to accurately determine this response was to put a speaker in an anechoic chamber, thereby avoiding room reverberations. Fortunately, there are now several tools that will enable you to make reliable measurements.

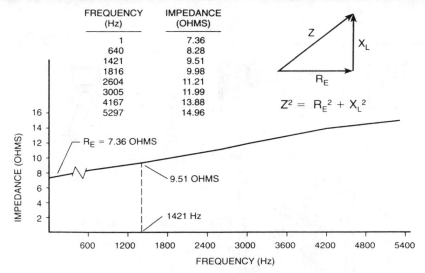

FREQUENCY (Hz)	IMPEDANCE (OHMS)
1	7.36
640	8.28
1421	9.51
1816	9.98
2604	11.21
3005	11.99
4167	13.88
5297	14.96

$$Z^2 = R_E^2 + X_L^2$$

Figure 2-8. Inductance of a Voice Coil

Far-Field Measurement

The critical tool is a warble tone generator which sweeps through 1/3 octave bands between 16 Hz and 20 kHz. The sweep at any one place is rapid enough so that the measuring system averages the response, thereby converging on the actual response instead of including the room reflection. The test setup is shown in *Figure 2-9*. The equipment needed to measure frequency response consists of:

1. A warble tone generator.
2. An audio amplifier.
3. The driver being tested (mounted on a baffle).
4. Several thick fiberglass sections.
5. A microphone (with a built-in analog or digital display sound-level meter, or connected to a separate AC voltmeter with dB scales).
6. A camera or mike stand to support the microphone/sound-level meter.

To measure frequency response in the range of 400 Hz to 20 kHz, place the microphone 19" to 39" away from the driver, on the center axis of the driver. This is called a *far-field measurement*. To avoid wall reflections, stay toward the center of the room. Place the fiberglass sections, as shown in *Figure 2-9*, on the floor between the driver and the microphone to suppress floor reflections.

Near-Field Measurement

A second method is used to measure the frequency response of a woofer from 20 Hz to 400 Hz. This time, place the microphone less than 1/2" from the center of the cone to avoid standing wave difficulties which typically occur at low frequencies. This is called a *near-field measurement*. As you vary the frequency, record the response in dB, using the data to later make a chart. Many electronics parts stores carry microphones housed with analog display sound-level meters, or digital display sound-level meters. These meters often use an OSHA-type microphone which

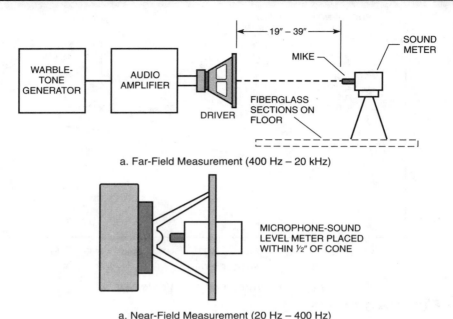

a. Far-Field Measurement (400 Hz – 20 kHz)

a. Near-Field Measurement (20 Hz – 400 Hz)

Figure 2-9. Test Setup to Measure Driver Frequency Response

is accurate to 9000 Hz, after which its ability to read higher frequencies rapidly falls off. Measuring accurately to 20 kHz may require more specialized microphones that must be matched to an AC voltmeter having dB scales. Warble-tone generators can often be found either in kit form or in partially-assembled form (a *metal chassis* must be used for proper operation of this generator).

PC SOFTWARE

For those of you who have a computer of the XT or AT class (or better) with at least EGA graphics capability, there is a reasonably priced hardware-software combination package that can perform tests for the impedance curve, FS, QTS and VAS very quickly. It is called *The Woofer Tester* and is available from C&S Audio Labs[2]. The hardware consists of a small AC powered "black box," which you connect to the COM 1 or COM 2 port of your computer. The black box communicates with the matching software that you install on your hard disk. If both of your COM ports are being used by devices, such as a mouse and a fax-modem, you can simply remove the mouse cable *after booting up* and plug in the 9-pin cable from the black box. The two test probes from the black box connect to the positive and negative terminals of the driver being tested. An impedance curve is created and F_S and Q_{TS} are found in a few minutes. Then, on a second run, you place nickels on the cone, tell the software how many nickels you used along with the driver's diameter and V_{AS} is quickly determined. You can also run impedance curves on midranges and tweeters using frequencies up to 20,000 Hz.

---

[2] Contact information for all product manufacturers mentioned in this book is given in the Appendix.

The Sealed Enclosure

3

What kind of bass response would you like? This chapter will introduce you to equations that will help you successfully design sealed enclosures that reflect your preferences. You will be required to make choices indicating how you wish to balance the two interdependent elements which completely determine the enclosure's low-end sound. The two critical elements are the size of the box and the final Q_{TC} of the system. They will account for the ultimate bass response and transient response of your sealed speaker system. Once you have made your choice of either box size or Q_{TC}, you will use this value to solve a series of equations. With the results you obtain from solving these equations, you will be able to sketch a curve reflecting the shape of the bass response of your design, using the familiar x-y axes of coordinate geometry. This picture, along with the transient response that Q_{TC} infers, will help you to decide whether or not the design will indeed result in the bass you desire.

BASS RESPONSE CURVE

The enclosure equations will provide quantities that can be used to plot points for a bass response curve. The powerful analytical tool of sketching curves on the x-y axes was developed in 17th century France, by René Decartes and Pierre De Fermat. In both mathematics and philosophy, Decartes' idea was: "proceed from the simple to the complex." Solutions to the equations in this chapter will give us simple points and straight lines used to sketch the complex bass response curve. If we carry Descartes' idea to the extreme, we can approximate the curve by connecting the points with straight lines, as shown in *Figure 3-1*.

The vertical axis is the response of the driver in decibels (dB). The horizontal axis is frequency in hertz (Hz). Solving frequency equations will provide F_{RMAX}, the frequency where maximum response occurs, and F_3, the frequency where the response is reduced by 3 dB below the reference response line. Solving response equations will provide the magnitude of the reference response line and the value that F_{RMAX} rises above this line. F_3 will, by definition, locate a point 3 dB below this line. Since the bass response of a driver in a closed box drops at the rate of -12 dB/octave below F_3, we can find several points quickly once we know F_3, as shown in *Figure 3-1*. (Note: An octave below a given frequency is a frequency which is one-half of the given frequency. An octave above a given frequency is a frequency which is twice the given frequency.)

EQUATIONS FOR A SEALED BOX

The sealed or closed box, because of its relative simplicity, has long been a favorite of

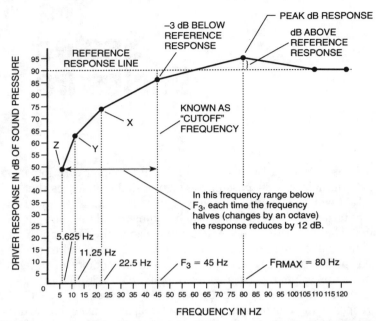

Figure 3-1. Sketching Base Response Curve Using Straight Lines

speaker builders. The heyday of the sealed box system took place in the 1950s, when Acoustic Research, the company founded by Edgar Villchur and Henry Kloss, began making "acoustic suspension" speakers based on Harry Olson's 1949 patent. This special type of sealed enclosure uses a *small* cabinet combined with a *highly compliant* woofer. The air enclosed in the small cabinet provides much of the stiffness needed for proper operation of the system and to prevent damage to the woofer, which it would sustain if driven in free air. The design, although somewhat inefficient, is still popular today.

The equations that we will use to predict a woofer's performance in a closed box come from the work of Dr. Richard Small[1] which was published in the 1970s. We will start the sequence of equations by finding the resonant frequency, F_{CB}, of the closed box speaker system. If you put a driver in a closed box, the driver's free air resonance, F_S, will rise to a higher frequency, F_{CB}. The reason why this happens is illustrated in *Figure 3-2*.

In free air, the driver has a compliance V_{AS} (represented in the spring as k). An enclosed volume of air, V_B, also has a compliance which can be represented in another spring by k'. Since this is air, there is no mass attached to this spring. When the driver is placed in the box, k and k' combine to form k''. This spring is stronger than either of the two that make it up. Since the driver in a box (i.e., the complete speaker system) has a higher stiffness (k''), it resonates at a higher frequency.

NOTE
The equations in this chapter are solved by using a scientific calculator or a scientific calculator function found as an accessory on PC software.

[1] R. Small, *Closed-Box Loudspeaker Systems*, Part 1&2, JAES, Jan./Feb. 1973.

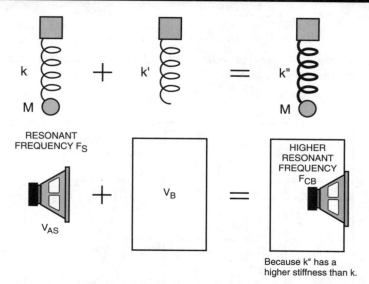

Figure 3-2. The Rise in Frequency from F_S to F_{CB} When a Driver Is Placed in a Closed Box

F_{CB}, the Resonant Frequency of a Sealed Box System

F_{CB} can be found by using the equation:

$$\frac{F_{CB}}{F_S} = \sqrt{\frac{V_{AS}}{V_B} + 1}$$

Let us return to the inexpensive polypropylene 6½" driver that we tested in Chapter 2 to see what happens when we try to put it into a compact sealed box. The following driver parameters were obtained from the tests made in Chapter 2:

F_S = 91.7 Hz	Q_{MS} = 5.15
S_D = 0.0139 M²	Q_{ES} = 1.61
V_{AS} = 0.326 ft³	Q_{TS} = 1.23

To begin evaluating the equation, we need to choose V_B, the internal volume of the box used for the enclosure. Let's use a compact internal volume of ½ cubic foot, or 0.5 ft³. Using this value, let's find the new F_{CB}.

With your calculator, begin by evaluating the simple statement *under* the square root sign on the right side of the equation:

$$V_{AS}/V_B + 1 = 0.326/0.5 + 1 = 0.652 + 1 = 1.652$$

The square root of 1.652 equals F_{CB}/F_S.

With 1.652 in the calculator's display, press the **INV** button (on some calculators called the 2nd function or shift button), then press X^2. This will give you the opposite of X^2 (i.e., the square root of 1.652) or 1.29. Since F_{CB}/F_S is equal to this square root, it tells us that F_{CB}/F_S = 1.29. Bring F_S to the other side of the equation by multiplying both sides by F_S, and you have:

$$F_{CB} = (1.29) \, F_S$$

Substitute 91.7 Hz for F_S:

$$F_{CB} = (1.29)\ 91.7 = 118.3\ Hz$$

Looking at *Figure 3-3*, you can now see the change to the impedance curve when a driver is put into a sealed box.

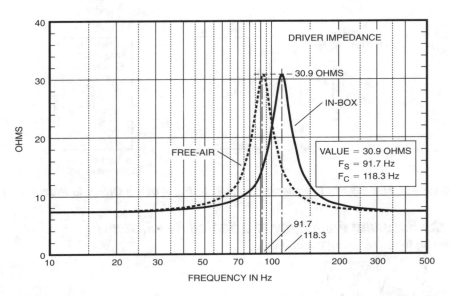

Figure 3-3. Change of Impedance of a 6½" Driver from Free Air to a 0.5 ft³ Closed Box

Q_{TC}, the Q of the Final Sealed Speaker System

Just as with F_S, Q_{TS} will rise to a higher value, Q_{TC} (the Q of the closed speaker system), when a driver is placed in a closed box. The right side of the equation used to find Q_{TC} is identical to the right side of the equation for F_C. The Q_{TC} equation is:

$$\frac{Q_{TC}}{Q_{TS}} = \sqrt{\frac{V_{AS}}{V_B} + 1}$$

This indicates that the final system Q will rise by the same multiple that F_C rose over F_S. The calculation will be easy, since we already know the multiple $[\sqrt{(V_{AS}/V_B + 1)}]$ = 1.29. Again, multiplying both sides of the equation by Q_{TC} solves for Q_{TC}:

$$Q_{TC} = (1.29)\ Q_{TS}$$

Since $Q_{TS} = 1.23$

$$Q_{TC} = (1.29)\ 1.23 = 1.57$$

This is considered to be a fairly high value. Looking back to *Figure 2-4*, you see that a Q higher than 1 clearly indicates that there will be a rise in the bass response of several dB. We see from *Figure 3-1* that the driver's response rises above the typical or reference response. Let's calculate this peak response in dB.

Peak dB, the Maximum Response

To calculate the peak response, we use the following equation:

$$\text{Peak dB} = 20 \times \log_{10} \sqrt{\frac{(Q_{TC})^4}{(Q_{TC})^2 - 0.25}}$$

Your scientific calculator will handle exponents and logarithms very quickly. *Don't be intimidated by this equation or any of the others that follow; it's just a matter of pressing the correct buttons.* If we again work from the simple to the complex, it would be best to start by calculating $Q_{TC}{}^4$, which is the same as $(Q_{TC}{}^2)^2$. On the calculator, just press the $\mathbf{X^2}$ button twice; this method is used in the following procedure. Here are the steps: (Be aware that in some PC calculators, multiply is * and divide is /.)

1. Enter 1.57 (which is the value for Q_{TC}) and press $\mathbf{X^2}$, and the calculator displays 2.4649.

You have calculated that $Q_{TC}{}^2 = (1.57)^2 = 2.4649$.

2. With 2.4649 in the display, press $\mathbf{X^2}$ again, and the calculator displays 6.06573. You have calculated that $(Q_{TC}{}^2)^2$ or $Q_{TC}{}^4 = 6.06573$ which is the numerator of the fraction under the square root sign in our equation.

3. Since the denominator under the square root sign uses $Q_{TC}{}^2$, which you know from step (1), then use it to calculate the denominator:

$$Q_{TC}{}^2 - 0.25 = 2.4649 - 0.25 = 2.2149 \text{ (the denominator)}$$

4. To save time, leave this number in the display and press the $\div$ button to divide by the numerator:

$$2.2149/6.06573 = 0.3651497$$

You say: "Wait, this is the wrong way, it should be numerator *over* denominator!" The scientific calculator has a wonderful $\mathbf{1/X}$ button which inverts fractions to save time:

5. With 0.3651497 displayed, press $\mathbf{1/X}$, and the calculator displays 2.738602.

This is the correct value of the numerator divided by the denominator; therefore, the value under the square root sign in our equation is 2.738602.

We now take the square root of this value using a two button sequence:

6. With 2.738602 displayed, press $\mathbf{INV}$ and then press $\mathbf{X^2}$, and the calculator displays 1.65487.

The square root of 2.738602 is 1.65487.

All we have to do now is take the logarithm to the base 10 of our answer and multiply by 20. (There are two common logarithm bases used in mathematics. We shall use the base 10 represented by **log**. The other is base e (approximately 2.718) represented by **ln**.)

7. With 1.65487 displayed, since we want base 10, press **log**, and the calculator displays 0.21876388

When you calculate the logarithm of a number you are actually finding an exponent. In this case, the base is 10, which means we have found the exponent such that $10^{0.21876388} = 1.65487$. The nature of our hearing has an exponential quality, which is why logarithms are often used in equations dealing with response in dB.

8. To complete the equation solution, press $\times$ **20** to multiply by 20, then press $=$, and the calculator displays 4.375.

This tells us the peak response is 4.375 dB, or 4.4 dB if we round it to the nearest tenth. Thus, we have just found that the response of this driver in a 0.5 ft³ closed box will go 4.4 dB above its reference response line.

F_{RMAX} – The Location of the Peak dB

The frequency at which peak dB occurs, FR_{MAX}, is determined by the equation:

$$F_{RMAX} = \left(\frac{1}{\sqrt{1 - \frac{1}{2(Q_{TC})^2}}} \right) \bullet F_C$$

This should be fairly quick, since we already know Q_{TC}^2 from step (1) of the previous calculation. Again, we will calculate what is under the square root sign first.

1. Enter the value for Q_{TC}^2 which is 2.4649. Press $\times$ **2** $=$ to multiply by 2, and the calculator displays 4.9298.

Since we want to know $1/2Q_{TC}^2$, we again use the **1/X** button to get the reciprocal value.

2. With 4.9298 displayed, press the **1/X** button, and the calculator displays 0.202847, the value of $1/2Q_{TC}^2$.

In order to evaluate the expression under the square root sign, $(1 - 1/2Q_{TC}^2)$, we need to subtract 0.202847 from 1 $(1 - 0.202847)$. The result in step 2 is positive, so we use another feature of the scientific calculator, the $\pm$ button, which will reverse the sign of a number.

3. With 0.202847 displayed, press $\pm$ and the calculator displays -0.202847

4. With -0.202847 displayed, press $+$ then press 1.

5. Finally, press $=$ and the calculator displays 0.79715 which is the result of adding 1 to -0.202847, or subtracting 0.202847 from **1**.

As a reference, we are now at the following point in the calculation: $F_{RMAX} = 1/\sqrt{0.79715}$

6. Press **INV** and then **X²**, and the calculator displays 0.8928336, which is the square root of 0.79715.

Again, the equation requires finding the reciprocal, which should now be familiar to you as the **1/X** button.

7. Press **1/X**, and the calculator displays 1.12, which is the reciprocal of 0.8928336.

Since this is the factor by which F_{RMAX} rises above F_C (previously found to be 118.3 Hz), we can now proceed to the final step in solving the equation, which is:

8. Press $\times$ **118.3** to multiply 1.12 by 118.3, then press $=$, and F_{RMAX} is displayed as 132.49 which, to the nearest tenth, is 132.5 Hz.

F_{RMAX} is the location where the response is 4.4 dB above the typical response. You can also expect frequencies around 132.5 Hz to be elevated as well. It is now fair to ask, "Just what is the typical or reference response of this driver?" Before we can answer this, we must first know the efficiency and the sensitivity of the driver.

THE EFFICIENCY AND THE SENSITIVITY OF A DRIVER

One of the common specifications given on the data sheet for drivers is what is known as a *power sensitivity* rating. For example, one 8-ohm driver may have a rating of 87 dB/1W/1m while a second may be rated at 90 dB/1W/1m. The meaning of 87 dB/1W/1m is that if you put one watt of power through the first driver and stand one meter away, the sound you will hear will have a response of 87 dB. The second driver will sound 3 dB louder under the exact same conditions, which means that it is *more efficient* at converting electrical power into acoustical power. In order to calculate the power sensitivity of our driver, we must first calculate its efficiency.

Calculating Efficiency, n_0

The equations described below assume the speaker is near a wall and that it disperses the sound into a hemisphere (sometimes called "half space" or 2π steradians). Since the equations use V_{AS}, we must make sure we use the correct equation for the units we are using. When we use V_{AS} in metric units, we must use the version of the equation for the driver efficiency (n_0) that uses V_{AS} in liters:

$$n_0 = 9.78 \times 10^{-10} \times V_{AS} \times F_S^3/Q_{ES}$$

When we use V_{AS} in English units, we must use the version of the equation that uses V_{AS} in **cubic feet**:

$$n_0 = 2.77 \times 10^{-8} \times V_{AS} \times F_S^3/Q_{ES}$$

We will use the latter equation since our driver's V_{AS} was calculated in cubic feet. We will calculate F_S^3 first. Recall that $F_S = 91.7$ Hz. Here are the steps:

1. Enter F_S as 91.7 so it is displayed in the calculator.

We shall now use a button that we haven't used before, the Y^X button. This button will raise a number, Y, to any exponent, X, that we wish.

2. Press Y^X and enter 3. Press =, and you have just found that $F_S^3 = 91.7^3 = 771095.213$.

3. Let us use the fact that 10^{-8} means move the decimal over eight places to the left. If we move the decimal of 771095.213 eight places to the left, it is just like multiplying by 10^{-8}, and we get 0.007710952. Make sure your calculator displays 0.007710952.

4. Now multiply everything in the numerator by the constant 2.77 and by 0.326 ft^3, which is the value of V_{AS}. Just press × **2.77** and × **0.326** and =.

$$(2.77)\,(0.326)\,(0.007710952) = 0.006963143$$

5. With 0.006963143 displayed, press ÷ **1.61** and = to divide by Q_{ES} (1.61) to find n_0:

$$n_0 = 0.006963143/1.61 = 0.0043249$$

Often n_0 is expressed as a percentage on specification sheets. To express our calculated value in percentage, we multiply n_0 by 100, or simply move the decimal value of n_0 two places to the right. This gives us $n_0 = 0.43\%$.

Calculating Sensitivity

We are now in a position to convert n_0 into a *sensitivity rating* using the equation:

$$\text{Sensitivity (dB)} = 112.2 + 10\log_{10}n_0$$

We continue with the steps:

6. Keep (or re-enter) the n_0 value of 0.0043249 in your calculator. Press **log** and =, which means you asked for the logarithm to the base 10 of 0.0043249. The calculator displays -2.3640. Press × **10** to multiply by 10 and the display is -23.640.

7. You can then find the final result for power sensitivity by adding 112.2 to −23.640. Press **+ 112.2 =**, and the calculator displays 88.559.

Power Sensitivity = 88.559 or, to the nearest tenth, 88.6 dB/1W/1m

Power Sensitivity is the Reference Response Level

The power sensitivity is also the reference response level, sometimes known as the *midband response*. It pinpoints the typical response of the driver well above resonance. In *Figure 3-1*, it is the response above 115 Hz. By using the midband response as a reference line, as shown in *Figure 3-1*, we can determine the value in dB of the peak at F_{RMAX} above the reference response level, and to identify the cutoff frequency, F_3, which is the frequency at which the sound pressure is −3 dB below the reference level. The cutoff frequency is regarded as an important marker because the bass quickly becomes inaudible below F_3, since it attenuates as −12 dB/octave.

Locating F_3 − Where Bass Response is Down −3 dB

Look at the equation below for F_3. It is a very nasty looking equation; however, you should have enough scientific calculator technique now to make short work of it. The equation to find F_3 is:

$$F_3 = \left[\sqrt{\frac{\left(\frac{1}{Q_{TC}^2} - 2\right) + \sqrt{\left(\frac{1}{Q_{TC}^2} - 2\right)^2 + 4}}{2}} \right] \times F_C$$

Since the expression $(1/Q_{TC}^2 - 2)$ appears twice, let us calculate it first. Here are the steps:

1. When calculating the peak dB previously, we found $Q_{TC}^2 = 2.4649$. Enter this value and press **1/X**. This tells us that the value of $(1/Q_{TC}^2)$ is 0.405695. Subtracting 2 (press **− 2 =**) we find $(1/Q_{TC}^2 - 2) = 0.405695 - 2 = -1.5943$. Record this value.
2. Since we need $(1/Q_{TC}^2 - 2)$ squared, press **X²**, and we find $(1/Q_{TC}^2 - 2)^2 = 2.5418$. Now add this quantity $(1/Q_{TC}^2 - 2)^2$ to 4 (press **+ 4 =**); it gives us 6.5418.

Recalling that $F_C = 118.3$ Hz, we can view the equation at this point as:

$$F_3 = \left[\sqrt{\frac{-1.5943 + \sqrt{6.5418}}{2}} \right] \times 118.3$$

3. With 6.5418 displayed, press **INV**, then **X²**, and the square root = 2.557695 is displayed.
4. Press **− 1.5943 =** to subtract 1.5943 from this square root and 0.963395 is displayed, and the equation reduces to:

$$F_3 = \sqrt{\frac{0.963395}{2}} \times 118.3$$

5. Divide by 2 by pressing **÷ 2 =** and the display is 0.4816975. Press **INV** then **X²** to obtain the square root of 0.4816975 and 0.6940443 is displayed. Multiply this quantity by F_C by pressing **× 118.3 =** and 82.1 Hz is displayed. We have found that $F_3 = 82.1$ Hz, the location where the response is −3 dB below the reference response.

We now have enough information to graph the results to form a complete picture. To summarize, we have calculated that for a sealed box of one-half cubic foot with a driver installed, the driver will have:

$F_C = 118.3$ Hz	Power Sensitivity = 88.6 dB/1w/1m
$F_3 = 82$ Hz	$n_0 = 0.43\%$
$F_{RMAX} = 132.5$ Hz	Peak dB = 4.4 dB
$Q_{TC} = 1.57$	

Picturing the Results

To graph the results and compare them to a solution that computer aided design software would generate, the initial parameters were put into TOP BOX, the software whose use is explained in Chapter 5. The graph that TOP BOX produced is illustrated in *Figure 3-4*. (Notice that the frequency scale is logarithmic instead of linear as in *Figure 3-1*. This causes the curves to look different.) Superimposed on top of this graph are dotted lines which, using Descartes' method, plots the results of our calculations on or near the curve. As you can see, the computer generated results and the calculations are in close agreement. The picture that has emerged of this moderately efficient 6½" driver, placed in a 0.5 ft³ box, delivers a clear message — do not expect *deep* bass (response drops at the rate of 12 dB/octave after 82 Hz) nor *sharply* detailed transients ($Q_{TC} = 1.57$). However, this inexpensive 6½" driver, along with a tweeter and crossover, could provide an *economical surround sound speaker system* in a relatively compact cabinet.

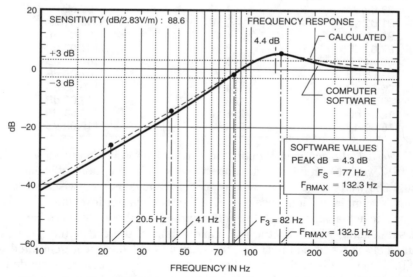

Figure 3-4. Base Response of a 6½" Driver in a 0.5 ft³ Closed Box Using TOP BOX

DRIVER SOUND PRESSURE VERSUS AMPLIFIER POWER

"How much power can these speakers handle?" This is probably the question most often asked by young speaker enthusiasts. Upon examination, you often find that they are really asking, "How loud can I play these speakers?" The sensitivity rating, not the power handling rating, is the guide to answering this rephrased question. The sensitivity rating is in decibels (dB). The decibel is a way of expressing the ratio of two powers, P_1 and P_2, according to the following equation:

$$dB = 10\log_{10}(P1/P2)$$

Now let's double the power of P_1 over P_2, and from the equation for dB we get:

$$dB = 10\log_{10}(2/1) = 10\log_{10}2 = 3.01 \text{ dB}$$

The equation illustrates that if you double the power from your amplifier (2/1), then an increase of 3.01 dB will occur. Normally this is approximated as 3 dB. As an example, let's see what happens when we input one watt of power, which produces 88.6 dB in the driver we are investigating, into another 8-ohm driver whose character-istic sensitivity is 92 dB/1W/1M, and then keep doubling the amplifier power to each. To give you a reference, since loudness is relative, normal speech is near 65 dB, a vacuum cleaner near 80 dB, rock concerts near 115 dB and pain at 130 dB. Let us look at rock concert levels shown in *Table 3-1,* keeping in mind that permanent hearing damage can happen, even though for a relatively brief exposure, at sound pressure levels less than 115 dB.

Table 3-1. Sound Pressure Output from Two Drivers as Amplifier Power is Doubled

Driver A	Power from Amp	Driver B
88.6 dB	1 W	92 dB
91.61 dB	2 W	95.01dB
94.62 dB	4 W	98.02 dB
97.63 dB	8 W	101.03 dB
100.64 dB	16 W	104.04 dB
103.65 dB	32 W	107.05 dB
106.66 dB	64 W	110.06 dB
109.67 dB	128 W	113.07 dB
112.68 dB	**256 W**	**116.08 dB**
115.69 dB	**512 W**	119.09 dB

As *Table 3-1* shows, even though the sensitivity ratings seem close, driver A demands 512 watts to produce rock concert levels while the more efficient driver B needs only 256 watts to give the same output. It is obviously far wiser to make the smaller investment in efficient speakers than the much larger investment in powerful amplifiers. The actual answer to "How much power can these speakers handle?" is a knotty issue dealing with both the mechanical limit of the driver (i.e., how far the cone can safely move in and out) and the thermal limit (i.e., heat generated in the voice coil). This issue is further complicated in that these limits are dependent both on the frequency being played and also whether one uses short transient power bursts or long duration power averages.

AN 8-OHM DRIVER VERSUS ITS 4-OHM TWIN

Drivers are sometimes offered in two impedance versions, identical except one is nominally rated 8 ohms whereas its twin is rated 4 ohms. A special case of this is the dual-voice-coil woofer. If you make connections to just one set of the two pairs of voice coil terminals, then the woofer is rated 8 ohms. However, if you connect both voice coils in parallel then, since $R_T = 8$ ohms/2, it becomes a 4-ohm woofer. The 4-ohm version has a different *voltage sensitivity* than its 8-ohm twin. To illustrate, let us first ask how much voltage is needed to produce 1 watt of power to an 8-ohm driver. This is an important issue, as modern day amplifiers are *constant voltage*, not constant power, sources. One equation for power is:

$$P = \text{Volts}^2/\text{Impedance}$$

Then 1 watt = $V^2/8$ and $V = 2.83$ volts. If this amplifier puts 2.83 volts into the 4-ohm twin, then $P = 2.83^2/4 = 2$ watts. From the preceding section, you saw that if you double the power from 1 watt (supplied to the 8-ohm driver) to 2 watts (fed to its 4-ohm twin), then you get a 3 dB increase in sound pressure. In other words, the 4-ohm driver is 3 dB more sensitive than its 8-ohm twin. What use does this have? If you intend to use a tweeter rated at 92 dB/1W/1m sensitivity and want to pair it with an 8-ohm driver rated 89 dB/1W/1m, try to find a 4-ohm twin of the driver. The sensitivity of the 4-ohm twin will be 92 dB, matching that of the tweeter. Another way to increase sensitivity is to use two identical 8-ohm woofers wired in parallel in the same enclosure. Each acts equivalent to a 4-ohm woofer and is 3dB more sensitive for a summed gain of 6 dB in sensitivity! We shall use this to great advantage later in a design that has come to be known as the *D'Appolito driver geometry*.

DESIGNING A PREFERENCE INTO A SEALED SPEAKER SYSTEM

The designer of a small "high-end" speaker company is a bass player and, of all preferences, the most important to him was to have a system Q_{TC} of 0.5. This seems a puzzle; a *bass player* designing a system whose *bass response drops* significantly by several dB even above F_3! However, he explained that he was accustomed to hearing the transients of an acoustic bass live, and this was what was most important to him. A $Q_{TC} = 0.5$, known as "transient perfect," gives the finest transient response but sacrifices a higher level of bass to achieve it. If you wish a $Q_{TC} = 5.0$, you must look for a driver with a $Q_{TS} < 0.5$, since Q can only rise in a closed box. A driver that meets this criteria, for example, would be a 61/2" polypropylene driver with the Thiele-Small parameters of $F_s = 50$ Hz, $Q_{TS} = 0.4$, and $V_{AS} = 1.5$ ft³. What size cabinet would be required to achieve a $Q_{TC} = 0.5$? The equation that we used to find Q_{TC}:

$$\frac{Q_{TC}}{Q_{TS}} = \sqrt{\frac{V_{AS}}{V_B} + 1}$$

can also be used to find V_B. Substituting the values we know and the Q_{TC} we desire gives us:

$$\frac{0.5}{0.4} = 1.25 = \sqrt{\frac{1.5}{V_B} + 1}$$

To solve for V_B, square both sides of the equation:

$$(1.25)^2 = (1.5/V_B + 1)$$
$$1.5625 = 1.5/V_B + 1$$

Subtract 1 from both sides:

$$0.5625 = 1.5/V_B$$

Solving for V_B, we arrive at:

$$V_B = 1.5/0.5625 = 2.66 \text{ ft}^3$$

If a certain value Q_{TC} is of paramount importance and you need to find V_B then, using the same steps, the original equation can be solved for V_B as:

$$V_B = V_{AS}/[(Q_{TC}/Q_{TS})^2 - 1]$$

Try this with your scientific calculator: You want to have the best compromise between bass response and transient response in your final design. A speaker system with $Q_{TC} = 0.707$ is considered to have the best balance between the two. You hope for a box size less than 2.66 ft³. Can this be achieved? Use the equation to find V_B **in cubic feet** to see if the box volume is acceptable. Your substitutions should be:

$$V_B = 1.5/[(0.707/0.4)^2 - 1]$$

Did you get 0.70619 ft³? If not, try again. To find the dimensions of the box, we'll use the acoustic ratio of 0.7937: 1 : 1.2599 that was presented in Chapter 1. First convert the volume to cubic inches (1 ft³ = 12″ × 12″ × 12″ = 1728 in³), which gives us (0.70619)(1728) = 1220.3 in³. Take the cube root of 1220.3 (most calculators require first pressing **INV** then pressing cube root). The result is 10.69″. This is the base dimension. The other two dimensions are (10.69)(1.2599) = 13.46″ and (10.69)(0.7937) = 8.48″. These are *inside dimensions,* so you must add the thickness of the material you use to build the box (1″ or 3/4″ being the most common) to each side to find the outside dimensions.

Increasing the Apparent Volume of the Box

When a sealed box is filled with either dacron (pillow stuffing) or fiberglass, it can serve to increase the volume of the box as the driver "sees" it. While it is clear that electrical and mechanical fundamentals are involved in speaker design, it is more difficult to realize that rules of thermodynamics also play a part. In an unfilled closed box, the driver changes the volume of air inside the box by compressing it, raising both the pressure and the temperature of the enclosed air. This is called an *adiabatic* process. If fiberglass is stuffed inside the closed box, then a large thermal mass has been added, which absorbs the heat that is generated by the system. This changes the system to an *isothermal* process in which temperature remains the same, and the equilibrium state under compression is more or less the same as the equilibrium state prior to compression. Since mass has been added to the system, the system's resonance is lowered. In practical terms, you can increase the apparent size of a box up to 15% using dacron and up to 18% using fiberglass. For example, if you stuffed the 1220.3 in³ box we needed to achieve a Q_{TC} of 0.707 in the previous section with fiberglass, then you could reduce the size to 1000.65 in³ box and have the same acoustical results. Let's call this new volume V_B'. It reduces the internal dimensions from 10.69″ × 13.46″ × 8.48″ to 10″ × 12.67″ × 7.94″. In terms of the amount of building materials and placement in small rooms where every inch counts, such a reduction can be useful. Standing waves inside the box would also be reduced.

The Vented Enclosure

In the 1920's, cities such as Memphis, Louisville and Cincinnati were famous for their jug bands. Performers in groups such as *Cannon's Jug Stompers*, *The Memphis String Band* and *Philip's Louisville Jug Band* mostly came from the rural south. They were used to improvising on any inexpensive portable objects that could make sound, such as washboards (still played today as the rub-board in Zydeco bands), washtubs (with broom handles and strings they became basses), spoons, combs, saws and jugs. When the musicians blew into the mouth of the ceramic jugs, they could imitate the tubas and trombones of jazz bands. The scientific term for the jug (when used to make sound) is the *Helmholtz Resonator*. The loudest tone is produced when the air masses that are suspended in the neck and body of the jug are set into resonance.

A PORT IN A CLOSED BOX

If a tube, or *port*, is put into a closed-box speaker enclosure, then it becomes similar to the jug and is now called a vented enclosure or box. At a certain frequency, called F_B, the woofer can put the air masses in the tube and the box into a common resonance. When you place a port in a closed box, you "tune" the box to a specific resonant frequency, F_B. At F_B, the air mass in the port vibrates *in phase* with the cone's movement, *damping* the cone's motion. The cone of the driver becomes virtually motionless and the sound comes primarily from the port. *Figure 4-1* illustrates the frequency response resulting from the driver (A) and the port (B) in a vented box. For the driver illustrated, the speaker system's response transfers from the driver (A) to the port (B) at 65 Hz. Notice that, at 43 Hz (F_B for this speaker system), the driver's response is at its minimum while port response is at its maximum. This is due to the port's damping action on the cone at F_B.

Even though the vented enclosure design dates from the 1930s, it was not until A.N. Thiele's 1962 article "Loudspeakers in Vented Boxes"[1] and R. Small's 1973 "Vented-Box Loudspeaker Systems"[2] were published that this design was given a firm mathematical basis. Their work was inspired by other men, such as J.F. Novak and L.L. Beranek, who had begun to model the vented box system as the mechanical equivalent of a high-pass crossover filter. A high-pass filter allows high frequencies to pass but blocks the low frequencies. *Figure 4-2* shows a mechanical model of the vented loudspeaker system.

[1] A.N. Thiele, "Loudspeakers in Vented Boxes," Journal of Acoustical Engineering Society (JAES), May-June 1971.
[2] R. Small, "Vented-Box Loudspeaker Systems," JAES, June-Oct 1973.

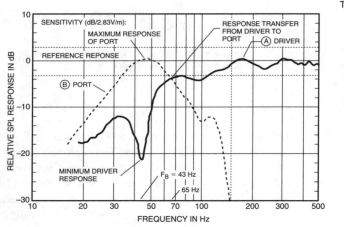

Figure 4-1. Driver and Port Response in a Vented Enclosure

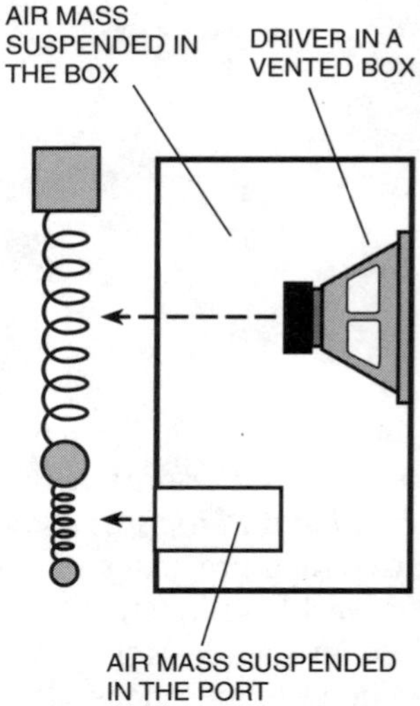

Figure 4-2. The Spring-Mass Mechanical Equivalent of a Driver in a Vented Box

Pros and Cons of Vented Enclosure

The mechanical model for a vented loudspeaker is a complex system composed of a small spring and mass suspended on a larger spring and mass. The smaller spring and mass represents the air mass suspended in the port. As the smaller spring and mass moves in phase with the larger spring and mass, it damps the motion of the larger system, so that only the smaller mass moves. The same happens to the driver at F_B. *Table 4-1* lists the advantages and disadvantages of a vented speaker system.

CHOOSING A DRIVER FOR A VENTED ENCLOSURE

Some drivers work better in a closed box, while others will give superior performance in a vented enclosure. The primary indicator of which box is best suited for any given driver is the *Efficiency Bandwidth Product*, EBP. The equation for EBP is:

$$EBP = \frac{F_S}{Q_{ES}}$$

where: F_S = free-air resonant frequency of driver in **Hz**
Q_{ES} = a number for driver's electrical damping control

A woofer that will work in a closed box should have an EBP less than 50. It should also have a Q_{TS} in the range $0.3 < Q_{TS} < 0.8$ and an ability for large cone movement (excursion, as measured by X_{MAX}). This means that, for woofers with diameters of 6 to 8 inches, X_{MAX} should be from 2 to 4 mm and for woofer diameters of 10 to 12 inches, X_{MAX} should be from 5 to 8 mm.

Table 4-1. Advantages and Disadvantages of a Vented Speaker System

Advantages	Disadvantages
1. The vented enclosure can be designed so that it is 3 dB more efficient than a closed box of the same size.	1. The vented box is more sensitive to "misalignments" than a closed box. Thus, when using a vented box design, you should definitely measure the parameters of the driver you intend to use and double check your mathematics.
2. Conversely, you can design a smaller vented box and get the same results as the closed box.	2. Misalignments can also occur because of air leaks in the box. The box should be well sealed with *no* gaps in the driver's mounting gasket. Use silicon caulking between the driver and cabinet as one way to prevent leaks.
3. For the same driver the vented box can be designed to have deeper bass, with an F_3 one-third of an octave lower than a closed box design.	3. The response of a vented enclosure falls at the rate of 24 dB/octave below F_3 as compared to the 12 dB/octave rolloff of the closed box. This gives a less favorable transient response to the vented enclosure which some people think is audible.
4. The reduced cone motion that occurs at F_B in a vented box reduces bass distortion, even up to an octave above F_B.	The dwindling group of people who still play records should have a "subsonic" filter in their receivers if they intend to use vented speakers. Since air is not trapped in vented speakers as it is in closed box speakers, a driver in a vented box encounters a decreasing air spring as frequencies dip below F_B. Vented speakers can thus be damaged by their excessive response to the extremely low frequencies coming from sources such as warped records.

A woofer better suited to a vented enclosure will have an EBP greater than 50, with best results if EBP is in the vicinity of 100. Q_{TS} should be in the range of 0.18 < Q_{TS} < 0.7 to obtain optimum response characteristics. To help you to choose the appropriate woofer for either type of enclosure, the relevant driver parameters are summarized in two tables. *Table 4-2* details the driver parameters as given on the original specification sheets supplied with the woofers. *Table 4-3* details the driver parameters as tested after a 60-minute break-in period using the tests described in Chapter 2.

EBP is calculated in both tables using the values for F_S and Q_{ES}. SPL is the sound pressure level. It has units of dB/1W/1m in *Table 4-2*, and has been converted to voltage sensitivity, dB/2.83V/1m, in *Table 4-3*. The voltage sensitivity in *Table 4-3* provides a more accurate comparison as modern day solid-state amplifiers are constant voltage output devices. The units in *Table 4-3* match the units required by the TOP BOX design software used in Chapter 5. L_{VC} in *Table 4-3* is calculated at 1kHz and given in millihenries as required by TOP BOX. Note that there are blanks in *Table 4-2* where no specifications were given. In addition, there also are variations in values between *Table 4-2* and *Table 4-3*, so to be as exact as possible in your design, measure the driver, if possible, to eliminate production variations. These tables also include additional parameters that will be used in the following chapters.

Table 4-2. Driver Parameters from Driver Specification Sheets

Driver (Radio Shack part number)	Remark	Q_{ES}	Q_{MS}	Q_{TS}	F_S	EBP	R_E	S_D [1]	V_{AS} [2]	X_{MAX} [3]	SPL [4]	P_E [5]
4" paper woofer (cat.# 40-1022B)	8 ohms	–[6]	–	0.35	55	–	–	–	0.23	–	84	10
6.5" polypropylene woofer (40-1011A)	8 ohms	–	–	0.4	50	–	–	–	1.5	–	92	50
8" polypropylene woofer (40-1024)	8 ohms	0.551	3.9	0.483	35	63.5	6.2	0.0206	2.1	0.343	86	50
10" polypropylene woofer (40-1014)	8 ohms	0.618	5.33	0.554	37	59.9	6.6	0.0354	4	0.25	91.5	50
15" polypropylene woofer (40-1301)	8 ohms	0.485	6.45	0.45	20	41.2	5.6	0.0856	21	0.347	90	100
8" dual-voice-coil subwoofer (40-1348)	single voice coil	0.6	2	0.48	45	75	8	0.0214	1.7	0.31	86	100
8" dual-voice-coil subwoofer (40-1348)	voice coils in parallel	0.6	2	0.48	45	75	4	0.0214	1.7	0.31	92	50
12" dual-voice-coil subwoofer (40-1350)	single voice coil	0.44	4.2	0.38	21	47.7	6.9	0.0532	13.3	0.46	89	120
12" dual-voice-coil subwoofer (40-1350)	voice coils in parallel	0.42	4.4	0.38	21	47.7	3.5	0.0532	13.3	0.46	95	60

Notes:
1. S_D is in square meters.
2. V_{AS} is in cubic feet.
3. X_{MAX} the maximum cone excursion, is in inches.
4. Power Sensitivity is in Sound Pressure Level (SPL) units of dB/1 Watt/1 meter.
5. P_E is in watts.
6. A – indicates no value specified.

Table 4-3. Driver Parameters from Measurements

Driver (Radio Shack part number)	Remarks	Q_{ES}	Q_{MS}	Q_{TS}	F_S	EBP	R_E	S_D [1]	V_{AS} [2]	X_{MAX} [3]	SPL [4]	L_{VC} [5]
4" paper woofer (cat.# 40-1022B)	single voice coil	0.647	3.55	0.548	91.7	141.7	7.15	53.52	17.77	3	93.3	0.88
6.5" polypropylene woofer (40-1011A)	single voice coil	0.959	3.42	0.749	57.8	60.3	7.65	129.86	26.49	4	88.4	.778
8" polypropylene woofer (40-1024)	single voice coil	0.649	5.16	0.577	40	61.6	6.3	206	64.24	8.7	90.1	1.65
10" polypropylene woofer (40-1014)	single voice coil	0.834	5.57	0.717	39.5	47.4	6.57	345	115.2	6.35	90.9	1.63
15" polypropylene woofer (40-1301)	single voice coil	0.575	7.14	0.532	22.4	39.0	5.72	856	547.7	8.8	92.3	2.52
8" dual-voice-coil subwoofer (40-1348)	single voice coil	1.59	2.78	0.967	51	32.1	5.07	214	40.47	7.87	88.6	.657
8" dual-voice-coil subwoofer (40-1348)	voice coils in parallel	0.796	2.78	0.619	51	64.1	2.65	214	40.47	7.87	94.1	.366
12" dual-voice-coil subwoofer (40-1350)	single voice coil	1.164	4.58	0.86	21.3	18.3	3.5	532	496.7	11.7	90.7	.976
12" dual-voice-coil subwoofer (40-1350)	voice coils in parallel	0.582	4.58	0.52	21.3	36.6	1.89	532	496.7	11.7	96	.4022

Notes:
1. S_D is in square centimeters.
2. V_{AS} is in liters. 1 liter = 0.0353 ft³.
3. X_{MAX} the maximum cone excursion, is in millimeters.
4. Voltage Sensitivity is in Sound Pressure Level (SPL) units of dB/2.83V/1 meter.
5. L_{VC} is in millihenries at 1kHz.

HOW TO DESIGN THE "IDEAL" VENTED ENCLOSURE

The task is to design a vented enclosure containing a driver. The first step is choosing a driver to fit into the general parameters we have defined for working best in vented enclosures.

Choosing the Driver and Desired Response

Let's choose a woofer from *Table 4-3*, since this gives us actual measured parameters. The 8" subwoofer has an EBP > 50 and a $Q_{TS} < 0.65$ when the two voice coils are connected in parallel. Since these values fit within the parameter criteria we defined, let's design a vented box with the voice coils coupled in this way. We want to design a vented box with a volume (V_B) that will give a *maximum flat response* (i.e., equal "loudness" at all frequencies). To do so, we don't first choose a Q_{TC} as we did for closed boxes; instead, the design steps call for us to solve a series of equations developed by D.B. Keele, Jr.,[3] using the vented enclosure alignments developed by A.N. Thiele. Keele's equations go further than Thiele's alignments in that they take into account real world losses such as air leaks from the enclosure.

Calculating V_B

The first equation is for V_B which determines the *ideal box volume* and is given by:

$$V_B = 15V_{AS}(Q_{TS})^{2.87}$$

where: V_{AS} = Volume in **ft³**
Q_{TS} = Total driver Q in free air

Since there will be conversions back and forth between the metric system and the English system, a table is provided in the Appendix to use whenever needed.

Here are the woofer's parameters from *Table 4-3:*

V_{AS} = 40.47 liters
Q_{TS} = 0.619
F_S = 51 Hz

Since V_{AS} is in liters, we must convert V_{AS} to cubic feet in the English system. Thus,

$$V_{AS} = 40.47 \text{ liters} \times 0.0353 = 1.4286 \text{ ft}^3$$

All values are now in the correct units so we can evaluate the equation $V_B = 15(V_{AS})(Q_{TS})^{2.87}$. The solution steps are:

1. Enter **0.619**, the value of Q_{TS}, into your scientific calculator. Press the **Yˣ** (Might be Xʸ on some calculators) button and enter **2.87**. Press = and the calculator displays the result of 0.2524365. You have just evaluated $(0.619)^{2.87}$ as 0.2524365.

2. With 0.2524365 displayed, press **X 15** = to multiply by 15. The calculator now displays 3.786547. Press **X 1.4286** = to multiply by V_{AS} in ft³. The calculator displays the ideal box volume, V_B = 5.409 ft³. To convert to cubic inches, multiply by 1728 by pressing **X 1728** = and V_B = 9346.75 in³.

---

[3] D.B. Keele, Jr., to authors' knowledge, never formally published these equations. They were circulated by letters to interested parties.

Calculate the box dimensions using the acoustic ratio as in Chapter 1. This is *not* a small box since, if you use 1″ cabinet walls, the external dimensions will be 18.7″ × 23.1″ × 28.6″. Let's find out if it is worth building such a big box by evaluating how this vented system will sound in the lower frequencies.

Calculating F_3

The next equation is used to evaluate F_3. Recall from *Figure 3-1,* that F_3 is the cutoff frequency of the bass response. The calculation of F_3 is made using the following equation:

$$F_3 = \frac{0.26F_S}{(Q_{TS})^{1.4}}$$

Start by bringing Q_{TS} into the numerator by making the exponent negative. This will make your calculations easier. The equation then becomes:

$$F_3 = 0.26F_S(Q_{TS})^{-1.4}$$

The solution to this equation is almost identical to the one for V_B. The steps are:

1. Start by entering 0.619, the value of Q_{TS}.
2. With 0.619 displayed, press $\mathbf{Y^x}$ and enter 1.4. Since you need −1.4, change +1.4 to −1.4 by pressing the ± button; then press =. The calculator displays 1.95719.
3. With 1.95719 displayed, press $\mathbf{X}$ **.26** = to multiply by 0.26. The result, which is displayed, is 0.5088695.
4. Finally, press $\mathbf{X}$ **51** = to multiply by the value of F_S. The final result is F_3 = 25.95 Hz.

This is indeed a low frequency; many people would trade the disadvantage of a large box for the ability to reach such deep bass sounds. We elect to make that trade, so we will continue the design. Since this is a vented enclosure, we must put a port into the box to tune the box to frequency F_B.

Calculating F_B

The equation for F_B is:

$$F_B = \frac{0.42F_S}{(Q_{TS})^{0.9}}$$

Again, to make the calculation easier, bring Q_{TS} to the numerator. Then the equation for F_B is:

$$F_B = 0.42F_S(Q_{TS})^{-0.9}$$

The same four basic steps are used to calculate F_B as were used to calculate F_3, except after the $\mathbf{Y^x}$ button is pressed, the exponent (X) is −0.9 rather than −1.4, and the constant multiplying factor is 0.42 rather than 0.26. The F_S remains 51 Hz. The answer you should get for F_B is:

$$F_B = 32.98 \text{ Hz or, to the nearest integer, 33 Hz}$$

Since the set of equations used is designed to give a maximally flat response curve, there is no need to calculate peak response. However, to complete the design, we must find both the diameter and the length of the port required to tune the box to 33 Hz.

Finding the Diameter of the Port Needed to Tune the Box

The port for a vented enclosure is usually made from some available tubing. The easiest ports to use are cut from circular PVC pipes. PVC pipes can be purchased with inside diameters of 0.5″, 0.75″, 1″, 1.5″, 2″, 3″, 4″ and 5″. Having selected the material, the next step is to select a diameter for the port. If the chosen port diameter is too small, wind noise from high-velocity air movement in the port is a likely possibility. In addition, at high-power levels, smaller ports cannot move adequate amounts of air, causing results to depart from what theory predicts. However, on the positive side, smaller port diameters require shorter tube lengths than larger diameter pipes. Since a port should not be closer than 3″ from a wall, a port diameter may have to be restricted to keep the length within reason. Conservative guidelines matching port diameters to drivers are given in *Table 4-5*.

Table 4-5. Guidelines for Matching Port Diameters to Drivers in Vented Boxes

Driver Diameter (Inches)	Port Diameter (Inches)
4	1
5 – 6	2
6 – 8	3
8 – 10	4
10 – 12	5
12 – 15	6

It is possible to use two or more ports, which combine to form the equivalent cross-sectional area of a single larger diameter port. Two circular ports of diameter D_A and D_B can be used as the counterpart of a larger diameter port D_C by using the following equation:

$$D_C = \sqrt{D_A{}^2 + D_B{}^2}$$

All diameters must be in the same units. Remember, the diameter chosen is an inside diameter.

Finding the Length of the Port Needed to Tune the Box

From the guidelines of *Table 4-5*, since we chose an 8″ driver, let's use a 3″ inside diameter port (radius = 1.5″) for the vented box. Once the diameter has been chosen, the next step is to calculate the length of the port needed to tune the box to F_B. Recall from our previous calculations that $V_B = 9346.75$ in³ and $F_B = 32.98$ Hz. We will use these values in the equation for the port length which will give us the result in inches. The length equation is:

$$L_V = \frac{1.463 \times 10^7 \times R^2}{F_B{}^2 V_B} - 1.463R \qquad \text{where: R = Port radius in \textbf{inches}}$$

$\qquad\qquad\qquad\qquad\qquad\qquad\qquad\qquad\quad V_B$ = Box volume in **cubic inches**
$\qquad\qquad\qquad\qquad\qquad\qquad\qquad\qquad\quad F_B$ = Tuned resonant frequency of box in **Hz**

In order to deal first with the simplest and then move to the complex, let's solve for the denominator first. The steps to the solution are:

1. Enter **32.98** for the value of F_B and press **X²** to display 1087.6804.

2. Press **X 9346.75 =** to multiply 1087.6804 by 9346.75 (V_B in cubic inches), displaying 10,166,276.78.
3. Divide the displayed number into 1 (bringing the number to the numerator) by pressing the **1/X** button, displaying 0.000000098.

We now have evaluated $1/F_B{}^2 V_B$.

4. With 0.000000098 displayed, press **X 10**, then press **Yˣ**, then press **7 =** and the display is 0.98.

These calculator actions have multiplied 0.000000098 by 10^7, thus moving the decimal to the right 7 places. The equation has now been reduced to $L_V = 1.463(1.5)^2(0.98) - 1.463(1.5)$.

5. With 0.98 displayed, press **X 1.5**, then press **X² =**, then press **X 1.463 =** to complete the first expression. The display shows 3.225915.
6. Press **− 1.463 x 1.5 =** to subtract the last expression, and the result for L_V is displayed as 1.031415 inches.

Converting to the nearest 32nd of an inch, $L_V = 1\tfrac{1}{32}$ inches. A summary of our results, designed to obtain a maximally flat response for this driver when installed in a vented enclosure is as follows:

$V_B = 5.4$ ft³	Vent Diameter = 3″
$F_3 = 26$ Hz	Vent Length = $1\tfrac{1}{32}$″
$F_B = 33$ Hz	

HOW TO CHANGE THE DESIGN TO A SMALLER BOX

It may be more important for you to have a smaller box than to reach down to 26 Hz. If this is the case, then let us begin this section by choosing a smaller V_B than ideal in order to see what will result. Let's say you have an old set of speaker cabinets that you would like to recycle. Each has an internal volume of $V_B = 1.05$ ft³. Starting with a given volume rather than calculating the ideal volume means that we must use a different set of equations.

Calculating F₃

This time we calculate the cutoff frequency F_3 first. To make an accurate comparison, we must use the same 8″ driver in this box. The equation for F_3 is:

$$F_3 = (V_{AS}/V_B)^{\frac{1}{2}} F_S)$$

Raising a number to the ½ is the same as taking the square root of that number, thus:

$$F_3 = \sqrt{(V_{AS}/V_B)} \times F_S$$

Using the previously established values of $V_{AS} = 1.4289$ ft³ and $F_S = 51$ Hz, we will calculate F_3. The solution steps are:

1. First evaluate V_{AS}/V_B. Enter **1.4289**, then press **÷ 1.05 =**. The result is displayed as 1.360857.
2. Take the square root of 1.360857 by pressing **INV** and then **X²**, which displays 1.1665578.

Now all we need to do to conclude the evaluation is multiply by F_S.

3. Press **X 51 =** and the display shows 59.49.

Thus, we have found that $F_3 = 59.49$ Hz.

Calculating F_B

We must now retune this new volume to a new F_B in order to achieve F_3. The equation to use for F_B is:

$$F_B = \left(\frac{V_{AS}}{V_B}\right)^{0.32} F_S$$

Here are the solution steps:
1. We know V_{AS}/V_B from the previous calculation to be 1.360857; enter this in the display.
2. To evaluate $(V_{AS}/V_B)^{0.32}$ press **Y^X**, enter **0.32** and press **=**. The result is displayed as 1.103621.

Now we can compete the evaluation by multiplying this value by the value of F_S, which we know is 51.
3. Press **X 51** and press **=**. The display shows 56.28.

Thus, we have found that $F_B = 56.28$ Hz.

Calculating a New Vent Length

Any change in volume or F_B means that a new vent must be determined. We need the port diameter and length. Let's keep the 3″ diameter we used previously and calculate a new vent length. We will use the same equation as before, so we will need V_B in cubic inches. We can find it by multiplying V_B in ft³ by 1728, thus:

$$1.05 \text{ ft}^3 \times 1728 = 1814.4 \text{ in}^3$$

We won't go through all the steps of the calculation because you use the same steps as for the previous solution, but here are some check points. First, we state the general equation for L_V, and then show it with all values substituted:

$$L_V = \frac{1.463 \times 10^7 \times R^2}{F_B{}^2 V_B} - 1.463R$$

$$L_V = \frac{1.463(10)^7(1.5)^2}{(56.3)^2(1814.4)} - 1.463(1.5)$$

Check to see that you get $L_V = 3.529202$ or $L_V = 3^{19}\!/_{32}$ inches.

As further practice, recalculate L_V if the vent diameter is changed to 2″. You should get a smaller L_V as compared to the length of the 3″ diameter port. Remember to *use the radius* of the port (R=1″) in the equation, *not the diameter!*

The Response Peak in a Smaller Box

When you change from the box volume which gives us a maximally flat response to a smaller box volume, invariably there will be a response peak. To find out how many dB's above the reference level this peak will be, use the following equation:

$$\text{Peak Response} = 20 \log_{10}\left[2.6(Q_{TS})\left(\frac{V_{AS}}{V_B}\right)^{0.35}\right]$$

where: $V_B = 1.05$ **ft³**
$V_{AS} = 1.4289$ **ft³**
$Q_{TS} = 0.619$

The solution steps are:
1. Enter **1.360857**, which is the previously calculated V_{AS}/V_B.

We need to evaluate $(V_{AS}/V_B)^{0.35}$.

2. Press Y^x and enter **0.35**, then press =. The displayed result is 1.11386965.
3. Press **X 2.6** = to multiply by 2.6. The display shows 2.896061.
4. With 2.896061 still in the display, press **X 0.619** = to multiply by 0.619 (which is Q_{TS}). The displayed result is 1.7926618.

This completes the evaluation of the expression within the brackets.

Now we must take the logarithm to base 10 of 1.7926618, then multiply by 20 to get the peak response value.

5. Press **log** and the display shows 0.253498. Press **X 20** and the display shows 5.06996.

Thus, we have found that the Peak Response = 5.07 dB

A Picture of the Results

To get a picture of the results of these calculations, the driver parameters were entered into TOP BOX, the software featured in the next chapter. One powerful feature of this software is that it can superimpose two curves on the same graph so that you can compare the results. *Figure 4-3* compares the deep and flat response produced with the driver in the 5.4 ft³ box tuned to 33 Hz (A), to the same driver in the 1.05 ft³ box (B). When using the software, you can move the crosshairs to any point on a curve so you can determine the response at any frequency. In the lower right-hand corner of *Figure 4-3,* two responses of the driver at the same position of the crosshair are given, corresponding to the two boxes in which the driver is placed.

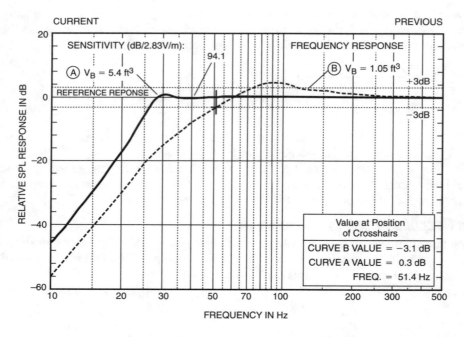

Figure 4-3. Comparison of Vented Enclosure Responses when $V_B = 5.4$ ft³ and $V_B = 1.05$ ft³ (Generated Using TOP BOX)

Computer-Aided Speaker Design 5

Our objective in this chapter is to demonstrate the use of available PC software to design speaker enclosures. In previous chapters, we have demonstrated that enclosure designs can be implemented by using a scientific calculator. With the use of PC software, the calculation task is eliminated, and it is much easier to accomplish "what-if" situations. It is not our objective to promote or endorse a particular software. We chose software that is reasonably priced and serves our purpose of easily demonstrating how software can be used for enclosure design.

TOP BOX SOFTWARE

TOP BOX is priced at less than $100.00, a fair price for a software program with its capabilities. It can quickly perform some very powerful calculations to place drivers in a box of the correct size to meet specific design goals. It is so easy to use that the manual is almost unnecessary. It has, in our opinion, what all software should have---a good user interface. The calculations we performed for the closed and vented box using the scientific calculator seemed to exhaust every conceivable design feature, yet TOP BOX executes many additional sophisticated computations. For example, TOP BOX takes into consideration the additional mass load that is placed on a driver from the air in the box which can, for larger drivers, add as much as 10% to the cone mass. TOP BOX also calculates the *voltage* sensitivity of a driver, rather than the less informative *power* sensitivity. This allows a direct comparison between the efficiency of two different designs.

TOP Box is available for either IBM™ compatible PCs or Macintosh® (MAC) computers. The MAC version can use both English and metric measurements, while the PC version uses metric only. The MAC version can overlay six designs; the PC version can overlay only two. If you use the PC version, you will probably need an English-to-metric conversion chart. As noted in Chapter 4, we have provided an abbreviated one in the Appendix. You will also use *Tables 4-2* and *4-3*, which summarize the parameters of commonly available drivers. The values in these tables are in metric values that can be input directly into TOP BOX.

Equipment Requirements

Table 5-1 identifies the *minimum* requirements for PC equipment to run TOP BOX. There should be little difficulty finding the equipment with adequate capability.

Table 5-1. PC Equipment Capabilities to Run TOP BOX

Equipment	Comment
PC	IBM™-compatible 286 (AT class) minimum
Graphics card	EGA/VGA, 512K Bytes minimum video memory
RAM	200K Bytes minimum free
Operating System	MS-DOS® 3.1 or above (not a Windows™ program)
Coprocessor	Not required
Disk Space	Can run from floppy disk. If installed on hard disk, need about 225K Bytes free space.

Installation Procedure

This procedure assumes that drive A is the 5¼″ drive[1] and that you will install TOP BOX on a hard disk designated as drive C. The installation procedure is as follows:

1. Boot the computer. At the C:\ prompt, type **MD TOPBOX** and press **Enter**.
2. Insert the TOP BOX 5¼″ disk in drive A.
3. Type **A:** to activate the 5¼″ floppy drive. Press **Enter**.
4. At the A:\ prompt, type **COPY A:*.* C:\TOPBOX** and press **Enter**. Remove the floppy disk after all files have been copied.
5. Type **C:** and press **Enter**. You should see the C:\ prompt.

TOP BOX VENTED-ENCLOSURE DESIGN

Let's now demonstrate a vented enclosure design using TOP BOX. The first step is to choose a driver. A 4″ paper woofer, listed in *Table 4-3*, stands out as a prime candidate for the vented box design. *Table 4-3* gives all of the Thiele-Small parameters in the proper units required by TOP BOX, except the power rating P_E which is given in *Table 4-2*.

Starting TOP BOX

To start TOP BOX, get to the C:\ prompt, type **CD TOPBOX** and press **Enter**. Then type **TOPBOX** and press **Enter**. The title screen appears. Press any key and the Option Selection screen appears as shown in *Figure 5-1*.

NOTE

*Make sure that **NUM LOCK** is off for all operations in TOP BOX.*

There are nine possible numbers you can enter in the **COMMAND** window, which is always displayed in the lower left-hand portion of the screen. Numbers 1-3 are used for **CLOSED BOX** designs, 4-6 for **BASS REFLEX** (vented) boxes, and 7-8 for **BANDPASS** subwoofers. Selecting number 9 for **QUIT** exits TOP BOX and returns to the root directory. The numbers 2, 3, 5, 6 and 8 are for designing driver enclosures to be used with an "equalizer," which is placed between the preamplifier and the amplifier.

Equalizers essentially are adjustable filters placed in the signal line to increase (boost) or decrease (cut) the signal response over a band of frequencies. They

[1] TOP BOX also available on 3½″ disk.

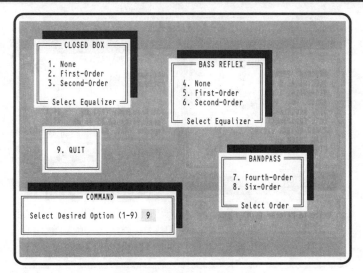

Figure 5-1. TOP BOX Option Selection Screen

usually have at least five band selections with boosts and cuts to ± 12 dB. Equalizers can perform feats such as reducing the low frequency peaking of a high-Q driver, controlling infrasonic cone motion, or boosting the low-end response over more than an octave. Some of the equalizers are passive, involving easy to make first- and second-order high-pass filters. They insert a variable loss of signal in the signal path. Other equalizers are active designs; they use operational amplifiers and transistors, and thus, add gain in the signal path. They are considerably more difficult to make. We will not discuss equalizer options in this book. If you are interested in these options, they are discussed in detail in the TOP BOX manual.

Since you are not using the equalizers, you will use only option numbers 1, 4 and 7. Let's say you want to design a bass reflex (vented box) driver enclosure. You type **4** in the **COMMAND** window and press **Enter**. TOP BOX immediately brings up the Driver Parameter screen similar to the one in *Figure 5-2, except the data fields are blank*, the **COMMAND** window prompt is different, and the **MESSAGE** window confirms the bass reflex selection.

Entering Driver Data

The **COMMAND** window asks, "Input Speaker Data File (Y/N)?" An "n" appears as the default answer. (TOP BOX presents the default answer that it expects you to choose.) TOP BOX is actually asking, "Do you have a data file stored with driver parameters that you want to retrieve for your driver data?" Since you want to input new data, you *accept the default* "n" by pressing **Enter**. TOP BOX then puts the cursor in the **DRIVER SPECIFICATION** window in the upper left-hand corner. You can now enter data from *Table 4-3* to fill TOP BOX's requests for information regarding the following parameters: F_S, Q_{ES}, Q_{MS}, V_{AS}, R_E, L_{VC}, P_E, X_{MAX} and S_D. For each parameter, type the value and press **Enter**. *Figure 5-2* shows the parameters for the 4" driver after they have been entered. Now we will go through a design to see how fast and easy it is. We will explain the subtle points later.

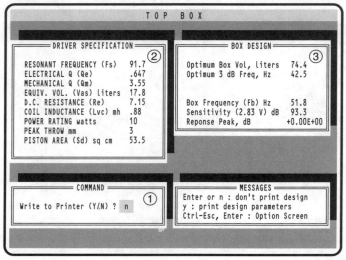

① Initial Screen has "Input Speaker Data File (Y/N)?"
② Initial Screen has all data fields blank.
③ Initial Screen does not show the BOX DESIGN window.

Figure 5-2. TOP BOX Driver Parameter Screen

1. The **COMMAND** window now asks, "Are These Values Correct (Y/N)?"
2. Double check the values you entered. If correct, accept the default "y" by pressing **Enter**.
3. The **COMMAND** window now asks, "Save Speaker Data File (Y/N)?"
4. This time do not accept the default "n"; type **y**.

This means you are going to save the data just entered on either the hard disk or on a floppy disk. For the sake of illustration, let's assume you want to save the data on a 3.5″ floppy disk.

Saving Data

5. In the **COMMAND** window, "A:\" is blinking. Your computer is configured so that drive B is a 3.5″ drive, so put a formatted 3.5″ floppy disk in drive B.
6. Type **B:** and press **Enter**. The **COMMAND** window now shows B:*.SPK.
7. TOP BOX is requesting that you type a name for the file you are about to save and use the extension .SPK. You choose 4SVC because this is a 4″ driver with a Single Voice Coil.
8. Type **4SVC.SPK** and press **Enter**.

Designing the Box

9. The **COMMAND** window now asks, "Design Box (Y/N)?"
10. Accept the default "y" by pressing **Enter**.
11. In the **BOX DESIGN** window in the upper right-hand corner, the values for the optimum box volume and the optimum F_3 appear. TOP BOX always begins the box design by giving you the box that produces the optimum results. This allows you to compare any changes you make later to the best that can be obtained with this particular driver. As shown in *Figure 5-2,* the

optimum volume for the 4" driver is 74.4 liters. Although this is large for a 4" driver, let us continue to consider it.

12. The **COMMAND** window now asks, "Is the Volume OK (Y/N)?"

13. Accept the default "y" by pressing **Enter**.

The bottom portion of the **BOX DESIGN** window shows the design values for the box frequency (F_B), the system's voltage sensitivity, and the response peak. In this optimum design, the response peak is and should be zero for a maximally flat design. The voltage sensitivity, in dB/2.83V/1m, is shown as 93.3 dB. The frequency to which the vented box should be tuned, F_B, is 51.8 Hz.

14. The **COMMAND** window now asks, "Write to Printer (Y/N)?" as shown in *Figure 5-2*.

15. Accept the default "n" by pressing **Enter**.

16. The **COMMAND** window now asks, "Design Port (Y/N)?

17. Accept the default "n" by pressing **Enter**.

Since "n" defaults are given, you can see that TOP BOX does not encourage you to print the results nor to design a port yet. Why? Because you may decide to change or abandon this design after viewing the results in graphic form.

18. The **COMMAND** window now asks, "Another Box Design (Y/N)?"

19. Accept the default "n" by pressing **Enter**.

20. The **COMMAND** window now asks, "Are These Values Correct(Y/N)?"

21. Accept the default "y" by pressing **Enter**.

Reviewing Initial Results — Response

TOP BOX displays **SCREEN 1** as shown in *Figure 5-3,* which is the first of three screens showing the calculated data. You can press the space bar to cycle through **SCREEN 2** and **SCREEN 3** and back to **SCREEN 1**. If you want to keep a record of this information, you can print out a hard copy. However, it is easier to analyze when viewed in graphic form, so let's do that.

```
============================= SCREEN 1 =============================
 Frequency    Response    Max Output     Max Input      Impedance
   (Hz)       (dB) [1]    SPL (dB) [2]   Pwr (W) [3]    Z (ohms) [4]
   10.00       -64.25       24.25          0.37           7.19
   10.80       -61.52       26.98          0.37           7.20
   11.70       -58.66       29.83          0.37           7.21
   12.60       -56.00       32.48          0.37           7.22
   13.60       -53.25       35.22          0.37           7.23
   14.70       -50.42       38.03          0.37           7.24
   15.90       -47.55       40.88          0.37           7.26
   17.70       -43.59       44.83          0.36           7.29
   18.50       -41.93       46.47          0.36           7.31
   20.00       -38.99       49.39          0.36           7.34
   21.60       -36.04       52.31          0.36           7.39
   23.30       -33.07       55.24          0.36           7.44
   25.20       -29.94       58.34          0.35           7.52
   27.20       -26.80       61.44          0.35           7.63
   29.40       -23.50       64.70          0.35           7.79
   31.70       -20.17       67.99          0.34           8.04
   34.30       -16.51       71.63          0.34           8.51
=============== Space for SCREEN 2, Enter to continue ===============
```

Figure 5-3. TOP BOX SCREEN 1 – Design Results in Tabular Form

22. To view the data in graphic form, press **Enter**.

TOP BOX displays a selection screen titled **SCREEN 1**, as shown in *Figure 5-4,* with the numbers [1], [2], [3], [4] in the column heads blinking and the **COMMAND** window prompts, "Select plot (1-4), 5=none". You type the number of the parameter that you want to view in graphic form. The selections are: [1] Frequency Response, [2] Maximum Output, [3] Maximum Input Power, [4] Impedance

23. Type **1** to view the frequency response of the driver.

The graphics screen appears. It is similar to *Figure 5-5* except the background is black, the grid is white, and the response curve is green. The response is plotted from +20 dB to −60 dB for the frequency range from 10 to 500 Hz.

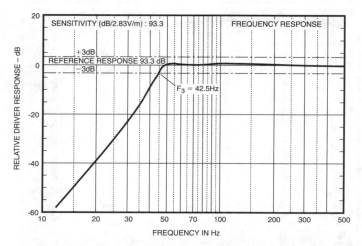

Frequency (Hz)	Response (dB)≘[1]≘	Max Output SPL (dB)≘[2]≘	Max Input Pwr (W)≘[3]≘	Impedance Z (ohms)≘[4]≘
10.00	−64.25	24.25	0.37	7.19
10.80	−61.52	26.98	0.37	7.20
11.70	−58.66	29.83	0.37	7.21
12.60	−56.00	32.48	0.37	7.22
13.60	−53.25	35.22	0.37	7.23
14.70	−50.42	38.03	0.37	7.24
15.90	−47.55	40.88	0.37	7.26
17.70	−43.59	44.83	0.36	7.29
18.50	−41.93	46.47	0.36	7.31
20.00	−38.99	49.39	0.36	7.34
21.60	−36.04	52.31	0.36	7.39
23.30	−33.07	55.24	0.36	7.44

Select Plot (1-4), 5=none 1

Base Reflex Configuration
Ctrl-H for Help

Figure 5-4. TOP BOX Selection Screen for Graphic Views

SENSITIVITY (dB/2.83V/m) : 93.3   FREQUENCY RESPONSE

+3dB
REFERENCE RESPONSE 93.3 dB
−3dB

F_3 = 42.5Hz

Figure 5-5. Driver Response (Maximally Flat Design) – Initial Results Using TOP BOX

Let's assume you want to know the exact response between 35 and 45 Hz. How does TOP BOX help you? Your PC keyboard has four arrow keys. If you press and hold down the left arrow key, (there may be a slight delay) you will see a crosshairs cursor enter the screen from the right-hand side and move along the response curve from right to left. As the crosshairs move, the exact response in dB for each frequency appears in a box on the bottom right of the screen. This was shown in *Figure 4-3*. Keep the left arrow key depressed until the crosshairs reach the band of frequencies in which you are interested. (You can also move the crosshairs to the right by holding down the right arrow key.)

The horizontal dotted lines above and below the 0 dB line are markers for +3 dB above the reference level and for −3 dB below. The intersection of the response curve and the lower dotted line is F_3. If you want a closer look, press the **Alt** and **1** keys simultaneously and the vertical scale (dB) expands so that the range is from 10 dB to −30 dB. Again press the **Alt** and **1** keys simultaneously and the vertical scale expands even more. Press **1** to return to the original vertical scale. *Figure 5-5* indicates that you can get good bass response from this 4″ driver, but you must use a large box. In summary, the design results are:

V_B = 74.4 liters = 2.63 ft^3
F_3 = 42.5 Hz
Power Sensitivity = 93.3 dB/2.83V/m
F_B = 51.8 Hz (frequency to which box is tuned)

Examining Other Results

Additional system parameters 2, 3, or 4 from **SCREEN 1** can be examined.

24. Press **Esc** or **space bar** and TOP BOX returns to **SCREEN 1**.
25. Press **Enter** and type **2** to plot the maximum output.

Maximum Output

The maximum output, shown in *Figure 5-6,* appears. It plots, up to a frequency of 500 Hz, the loudest response (in dB) the designed speaker system can play. It tells us that the maximum output from the system is 103 dB above 175 Hz. At 175 Hz, the maximum output begins dropping, and at 73 Hz, it has dropped 9 dB to an output level of 94 dB. Although not rock concert levels, this is nonetheless quite loud! After 50 Hz, the ability to give a loud bass response descends rapidly, so that frequencies below 30 Hz would be considered inaudible even at maximum output.

Maximum Input Power

We would like to answer the question we asked in Chapter 3: "How much power can a speaker system handle?" We need to examine the maximum input to help us obtain the answer.

26. Press **Esc** and TOP BOX returns to **SCREEN 1**.
27. Press **Enter** and type **3** to plot the maximum input.

The maximum input power is displayed as shown in *Figure 5-7.* Recall that when you entered data for the **DRIVER SPECIFICATION** window *(Figure 5-2)*, you entered 10 watts for the power rating (P_E), which you obtained from *Table 4-3. Figure 5-7* shows that this speaker system can take 10 watts only from 500 Hz to about 175 Hz. Below 175 Hz, the curve rapidly descends to only a few watts below 100 Hz. What

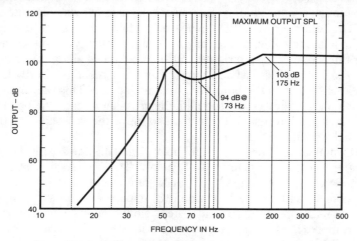

Figure 5-6. Maximum Output SPL Using TOP BOX

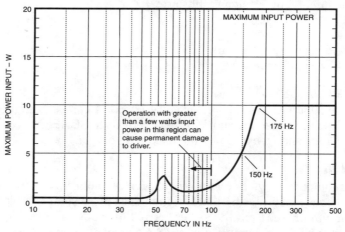

Figure 5-7. Maximum Input Power in Watts Using TOP BOX

this means is that if the volume is turned up for more bass, and your amplifier is delivering more than 5 watts to the speaker system below 150 Hz, you are exceeding X_{MAX} and, with increasing power, you are most likely exceeding the thermal limit of the speaker as well. Such operation can lead to permanent damage of the driver.

Impedance

Let's now examine the impedance of the driver in the vented enclosure.

28. Press **Esc** and TOP BOX returns to **SCREEN 1**.

29. Press **Enter** and type **4** to plot impedance.

The speaker impedance curve of your vented box system is displayed as shown in *Figure 5-8*. Compare this impedance to the impedance curve of a closed box system as shown in *Figure 3-3*. Clearly, the vented box system has an impedance curve with two "hills" as compared to the single "mountain" of the closed box system. The mind's eye could almost visualize a finger pushing down on the maximum point at the top of the closed box's impedance curve, creating two hills on either side. In a sense, this is what happens. The vented box is tuned to 51.8 Hz, which renders the cone nearly motionless at that frequency. *Maximum impedance* in the closed box was due to the very *energetic motion of the cone* at resonance. The vented box has *minimum cone motion* at F_B, the box resonant frequency to which the port tuned the box, producing *minimum impedance* at that point. Since modern amplifiers are constant voltage devices, the two "hills" are no more difficult for the amplifier to surmount than the single "mountain" of the closed box.

30. Press **Ctrl** and **Esc** at the same time to return to the Option Selection screen. If you want to quit TOP BOX, press **9**.

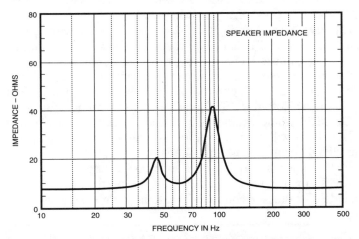

Figure 5-8. Impedance of Vented Box Design Using TOP BOX

ANOTHER DESIGN – SAME DRIVER

Let's say you want to do another design using the same driver, but this time with a smaller box. We will show the design steps. If you have already quit TOP BOX, start it again.

1. On the Option Selection screen *(Figure 5-1)*, press **4**. In the **COMMAND** window, TOP BOX asks, "Input speaker data file (Y/N)?". Type **y** so you can retrieve the data you saved on a floppy disk.
2. A blinking "B:*.SPK" appears. Insert the 3.5″ floppy disk that contains your previously saved speaker file into drive B. Press **Enter** and TOP BOX presents a list of all the speaker files you have saved to this directory so that you can choose one.
3. File name 4SVC.SPK is listed and highlighted. Press **Enter**.

TOP BOX retrieves the information saved on the floppy and places it into the **DRIVER SPECIFICATION** box.

4. The **COMMAND** window now asks, "Are These Values Correct(Y/N)?"
5. Accept the default "y" by pressing **Enter**.
6. The **COMMAND** window now asks, "Design Box (Y/N)?"
7. Accept the default "y" by pressing **Enter**.

The same optimum box volume and F_3 appear in the **BOX DESIGN** window as before.

8. The **COMMAND** window now asks, "Is the volume OK (Y/N)?" Type **n** so that you can change the volume.

Choosing New Box Volume

TOP BOX places the cursor in the **BOX DESIGN** window so you can type the desired V_B. Since your objective is a smaller box than the optimum 74.4 liters (2.63 ft³), you will change V_B to 15 liters (0.53 ft³) for the new design.

9. Type **15** after "Box Volume (Vb) liters" and press **Enter**.

As shown in *Figure 5-9*, the **BOX DESIGN** window displays F_3 = 85.8 Hz.

10. For "Is F3 OK?", press **Enter** to accept "y".

Now the **BOX DESIGN** window displays F_B = 83.9 Hz, Sensitivity (2.83 V) = 93.3 dB, and Response Peak = 4.36 dB. Since you specified a smaller box volume, instead of a maximally flat design, there is a peak in the response curve.

11. For "Write to Printer?", press **Enter** to accept "n".

12. For "Design port?", type **y** so that you may see this phase of the design.

13. For "Round or Slotted (R/S)?", type **r** because a round PVC tube will be used.

The **PORT DESIGN** window appears in the lower right-hand corner as shown in *Figure 5-9*. TOP BOX will model a vented system which may have one or several ports. This modified design will use only one port.

14. For the "Number of Ports", type **1** and press **Enter**.

15. TOP BOX now requests "Diameter (of the port) in cm." *Table 5-2* converts the inside diameters of common PVC tubing from inches to centimeters.

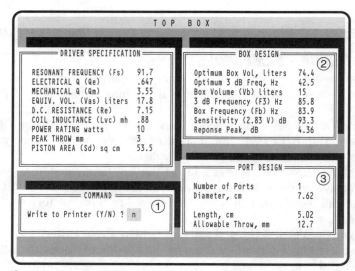

① Questions asked in COMMAND window as design progresses.
② New lines and new values change as new volume is selected.
③ PORT DESIGN window appears as design proceeds.

Figure 5-9. Driver Parameter Screen Showing a New BOX DESIGN Window and PORT DESIGN Window

Table 5-2. Conversion of Diameters from Inches to Centimeters

Inside Diameter (inches)	Diameter (centimeters)
0.5	1.27
1	2.54
1.5	3.81
2	5.08
3	7.62
4	10.16
5	12.7

16. Our choice is a 1″ diameter tube. At the "Diameter, cm" prompt, type **2.54** and press **Enter**.

TOP BOX flashes a message, "Length < 0, Increase Port Area." Because small diameter tubes produce shorter lengths, sometimes the length is too short for the thickness of the box material, which is often 3/4″. Increasing the port diameter will produce a longer port length. Recycle by choosing **Y** at "Design Port?"

17. Our second choice is a 3″ diameter tube. At the "Diameter, cm" prompt, type **7.62**.

This time TOP BOX accepts the diameter and produces the length which, as shown in *Figure 5-9,* is given as 5.02 cm. This is equivalent to 1.9864 inches or, to the closest 32nd of an inch, $1^{31}/_{32}″$.

Comparing Design Results

Let's compare the maximally flat design of the 74.4-liter box shown in *Figure 5-5* by overlaying it on the frequency response of the current 15-liter box design.

18. Press **Enter** to answer each of the questions until you reach **SCREEN 1** with the blinking numbers.
19. For "Save as previous case (Y/N)?", press **Enter** to accept the default "y".
20. For "Print results (Y/N)?", press **Enter** to accept the default "n." TOP BOX returns to the Option Selection screen *(Figure 5-1)*.
21. Choose option 4 again and go through the entire process, this time accepting the maximally flat design that TOP BOX displays in the **BOX DESIGN** window. You may design the port or bypass it.
22. When **SCREEN 1** with blinking numbers is displayed, press **1** to view the frequency graph.
23. For "Over Plot Previous Case?", press **Enter** to accept the default "y". Both frequency response curves are displayed as shown in *Figure 5-10.*

The frequency response curve of the 15-liter box shows an F_3 of 86 Hz. Now you can directly compare the two and ask yourself, "What is more important to me, a small box with limited bass response, or the deeper response of the bigger box?" If neither is satisfactory, you can easily try a new design simply by inserting new design values into TOP BOX. That's the big advantage of using PC software rather than a scientific calculator. Working with the computer provides nearly instantaneous results as compared to doing the computations on a scientific calculator.

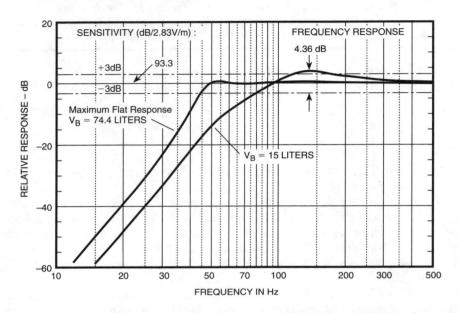

Figure 5-10. Vented Box – Comparing Maximally Flat Reponse (V_B = 74.4 Liters) with Smaller 15-Liter Box Design Using TOP BOX

SUMMARY

In this chapter, we demonstrated that PC software is easy to use and has the flexibility and speed to consider different design variables quickly. Although we used TOP BOX, other PC software packages are available that will provide similar results. We are not saying that you *need* PC software — we have already shown in previous chapters that you can do all of the calculations on a scientific calculator — but we wanted to demonstrate that PC software makes the task much easier.

In the following chapters, we will use TOP BOX to complete specific designs that you may use "as is" for building a system. Or you can use your PC software or scientific calculator to modify the presented designs to meet your specific requirements.

Subwoofers

6

Subwoofers are speakers that enhance audio response in the very low end of the frequency range — the bass region. The range of human hearing, which becomes more limited as we get older, extends from a lower threshold of 16 Hz to a high of 20,000 Hz. If we come three octaves down from 20,000 Hz, we are at 2,500 Hz, the high end of the midrange of the audio spectrum. If we go four octaves up from 16 Hz, we go through hundreds, but not thousands, of hertz, reaching 256 Hz at the low end of the midrange.

Very few instruments have their *fundamental* tone, the basic waveform known in music as the pitch, in the first few octaves of the bass region. The lowest note on the organ is 16.4 Hz, while the lowest notes on the piano, harp and contrabassoon are all closer to 32 Hz, the first octave up from 16 Hz. The double bass does not start until 41.2 Hz. While the lowest human bass voice may be capable of 87 Hz, in opera it is more typical for a bass singer to venture only near 128 Hz, the third octave up from 16 Hz. At the high end, the highest fundamental note comes from the piccolo, at 4186 Hz. This is not the upper limit of musical instruments, however, as the important *harmonics* produced by all non-electronic instruments are of even higher frequencies — as high as 16,000 Hz to 17,000 Hz for violins and cymbals. (Harmonics are integral multiples of the fundamental and are called *overtones* in music.) It is the unique spectrum of harmonics produced by each instrument that enables us to distinguish a violin from a clarinet when each plays the same fundamental note.

To further complicate matters, our ears are not nearly as sensitive to high or low frequency sounds as they are to the midrange, especially to those frequencies between 1000 and 2000 Hz. In fact, the purpose of the loudness control found on many receivers is to *boost* the low and high frequencies when music is played at soft levels, so that the ear hears these frequencies at approximately the same level as the midrange frequencies. If we are relatively insensitive to the lower segment of the musical range where so few instruments venture, then why all this obsession with the bass? Perhaps we consider bass so essential because it can make music a more visceral experience for us. As is sometimes the case when music is played near concert levels, bass can be *felt* almost as much as it can be heard. The subwoofer can provide much of the impact that people find missing when listening to a pair of speakers of small dimensions.

CONSTANT-PRESSURE ISOBARIC WOOFER DESIGNS

In order to "feel" the bass, a subwoofer has to move a lot of air. Let's look at a couple of designs of subwoofer systems. These designs are based on combining woofers into compound woofer pairs using a technique called *constant pressure loading*. A constant pressure loading design, alternately called *isobaric* (*iso* for constant, *baric* for pressure) was first described by Harry Olson in the 1950s, but was not used commercially until the 1970s. Such a design using a woofer pair is of interest because the box size can be reduced in half over a design using a single woofer. As shown in *Figure 6-1d,* it is the change in parameters as the design changes from a single driver to a compound pair that permits halving the volume.

Tunnel Enclosure

One way to implement the technique is to use two identical woofers acoustically connected by a very small tunnel enclosure as shown in *Figure 6-1b*. Electrically, the voice coils of these two woofers can be connected either in parallel or series. The small amount of air trapped between the two woofers acts as a very stiff spring which effectively connects the suspension system of the two drivers, turning the pair into a single compound driver. Since the two cones move together, the air trapped in the tunnel between is maintained in a state of constant pressure, hence the name.

Even though the piston area remains the same, the suspension systems of both woofers in an isobaric system are now *coupled*. It can be said they have *twice* the stiffness or, conversely, half the compliance, C_M, of the single driver. Since V_{AS} of a single driver is:

$$V_{AS} = 1.4 \times 10^5 \times C_{MS} \times S_D{}^2$$

and we call V'_{AS} the *new* V_{AS} for the compound pair and use the fact that C_{MS} is now one-half, then:

$$V'_{AS} = 1.4 \times 10^5 \times \tfrac{1}{2} C_{MS} \times S_D{}^2 = \tfrac{1}{2} V_{AS}$$

The compound driver's air compliance V_{AS} is one-half that of the single driver. If V_{AS} is halved, then the design equations for a closed box dictate that an enclosure half the size gives the same bass performance.

Since n_0 depends directly on V_{AS}, then n_0, the reference efficiency for the compound pair, is also *half that of the single driver*. However, if the voice coils of the compound pair are electrically connected in parallel, then R_E and L_{VC} are one-half the single-driver values and the compound pair becomes a 4-ohm version of the 8-ohm original. This gives a +3 dB gain in sensitivity, but since the reference efficiency of the pair is half that of the original driver, the end result is *no gain*.

Using the spring-mass equation for F_S, and substituting that C_{MS} is *half* that of a single driver while the mass M_{MS} of the system is *double* the single driver mass, M, because we have two cones, we see that F'_S, the resonance for the compound pair is:

$$F'_S = \frac{1}{2\pi} \sqrt{\frac{1}{\tfrac{1}{2}C_{MS}2M}} = F_S$$

or F'_S is the same as the original single driver's F_S. The parameters are summarized in *Figure 6-1d* compared to a single driver. We can further enhance the benefits of the isobaric pair by combining it with another technique known as push-pull.

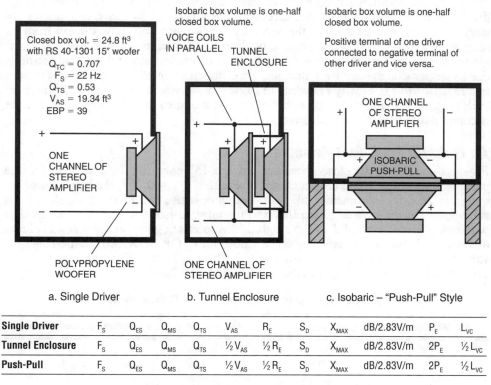

d. Constant Pressure Driver Parameters Compared to Single Driver

Single Driver	F_S	Q_{ES}	Q_{MS}	Q_{TS}	V_{AS}	R_E	S_D	X_{MAX}	dB/2.83V/m	P_E	L_{VC}
Tunnel Enclosure	F_S	Q_{ES}	Q_{MS}	Q_{TS}	$\frac{1}{2}V_{AS}$	$\frac{1}{2}R_E$	S_D	X_{MAX}	dB/2.83V/m	$2P_E$	$\frac{1}{2}L_{VC}$
Push-Pull	F_S	Q_{ES}	Q_{MS}	Q_{TS}	$\frac{1}{2}V_{AS}$	$\frac{1}{2}R_E$	S_D	X_{MAX}	dB/2.83V/m	$2P_E$	$\frac{1}{2}L_{VC}$

Figure 6-1. Constant Pressure Compound Drivers

Isobaric Push-Pull

The push-pull technique, used by itself, works by mounting two woofers on the same enclosure side, except that the direction of one woofer is reversed so that it faces into the enclosure. Such a mounting may raise some questions: "Won't the two cones now move in opposite directions? If so, won't the bass coming from one woofer *cancel* the bass coming from the other?" This is correct and, unless the *polarity* of one driver is reversed, expect the bass performance of the push-pull pair to be a calamity. To avoid this complication, you connect the positive (+) terminal (often marked in red) of the voice coil of one driver to the negative (−) terminal of the voice coil of the other driver and vice versa. The drivers are now wired electrically "out of phase;" however, now the cones of the drivers in this push-pull pair move in the same direction, making them acoustically "in phase."

If we use the isobaric technique in combination with the push-pull style, there is no need for the small tunnel enclosure to acoustically connect the two woofers. Instead, as shown in *Figure 6-1c,* one woofer is placed on top of the other so that they each face opposite directions. This eliminates building a small enclosure since, *if the circumference is properly sealed*, there will be a pocket of air trapped between the two drivers causing them to act as a compound pair.

There are additional benefits from using the push-pull technique. Even though the cones now move in the same direction, the voice coil in one driver moves *toward* its permanent magnet as the second driver's voice coil moves *away* from its magnet. The result is that asymmetric nonlinearities, such as those caused by a single voice coil moving through a magnetic field of uneven strength or nonlinearities due to suspension system irregularities, are eliminated. In effect, *second-order harmonic distortion* is greatly *reduced*. In *Figure 6-1d*, which uses identical drivers in each system, the parameters of a pair of drivers mounted in isobaric push-pull style is compared to that of a single driver.

An Isobaric Push-Pull Example

Figure 6-1a shows the closed box size using a 15" polypropylene woofer with the parameters shown. To achieve a closed box with a $Q_{TC} = 0.707$, the box volume required is 24.8 ft³---a considerable size. Let us now use two of these woofers for a subwoofer design---wired in parallel and mounted in isobaric push-pull style. The parameters from *Table 4-3* of the single 15" woofer are given in the second column of *Table 6-1*, but before entering these values into TOP BOX, we must change the values per the comparison for *Figure 6-1* (third column). The parameters to be used in TOP BOX are shown in the fourth column of *Table 6-1*.

Table 6-1. Converted Isobaric Push-Pull Driver Parameters

15" Woofer Driver	Original	Per Figure 6-1	Isobaric Push-Pull
F_S (Hz)	22	same	22
Q_{ES}	0.575	same	0.575
Q_{MS}	7.14	same	7.14
V_{AS} (l)	547.7	½ (V_{AS})	274
R_E (Ω)	5.72	½ (R_E)	2.86
L_{VC} (mH)	2.52	½ (L_{VC})	1.26
P_E (W)	100	2 (P_E)	200
X_{MAX} (mm)	8.8	same	8.8
S_D (cm²)	856	same	856

The isobaric push-pull parameters are entered into the **DRIVER SPECIFICA-TION** window as shown in *Figure 6-2*. Four of the nine single driver parameters have changed. TOP BOX tells us that a 415-liter (14.7 ft³) box gives us an optimum flat response design with $Q_{TC} = 0.71$. This box size is approximately half the box size needed when using a single woofer (24.8 ft³). However, suppose you have available a 100-liter (3.5 ft³) box. If we enter this size box into our program, TOP BOX's screen, shown in *Figure 6-2*, tells us that this box design will have an $F_3 = 31.4$ Hz and $Q_{TC} = 1.06$, which produces a 1.63 dB response peak in the bass region.

These values indicate that a 3.5 ft³ box is a viable option when used with a compound pair, whereas the same box using a single woofer would not be. As theory predicted, the sensitivity forecast by TOP BOX in the **BOX DESIGN** window for the compound pair is virtually the same as that of a single 15" woofer. *Figure 6-3* illustrates the frequency response graph of the isobaric push-pull pair in a 3.5 ft³ (100 liter) sealed box. We will use these drivers in a 100-liter box, exploiting the isobaric push-pull design as part of a complete 3-way speaker in Chapter 8.

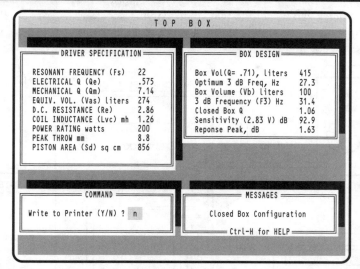

Figure 6-2. TOP BOX Closed Box Design with $Q_{TC} = 0.71$ (maximally flat) and $Q_{TC} = 1.06$ ($V_B = 100$ liters)

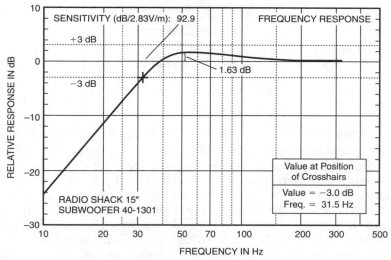

Figure 6-3. Closed Box Using 15″ Woofer in Isobaric Push-Pull with 100-liter (3.5 ft³) Box Size (Generated Using TOP BOX)

THE DUAL-VOICE-COIL SUBWOOFER

The dual-voice-coil subwoofer is a relatively new type of woofer which can be used as a subwoofer when paired with two satellite speakers. This modern breed of woofer has two voice coils, one wound directly with the other, and two separate pairs of + and − terminals, usually located on opposite sides of the driver basket. In all of our previous designs, each speaker was connected to only one channel of an amplifier. One of the notable features of this type of woofer is that the bass from both channels of the stereo amplifier can be fed into this single driver. Using a crossover filter, the higher frequencies can be sent to two small satellite speakers. *Figure 6-4* illustrates a dual-voice-coil woofer, mounted on the bottom of a subwoofer enclosure, in use with a pair of satellite speakers.

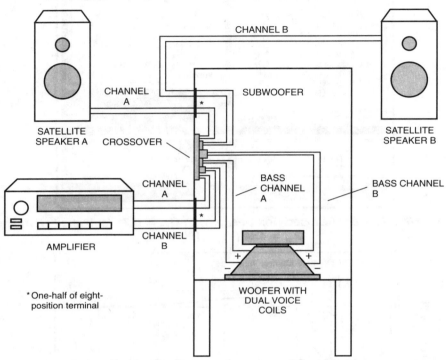

Figure 6-4. Dual-Voice-Coil Subwoofer with Two Satellite Speakers

One must be careful when reading the parameter specifications of dual-voiced coil woofers from "spec" sheets, as manufacturers have not developed a uniform method of making measurements. As we saw in Chapter 2, all woofers can be tested to measure the parameter Q_{ES}, which indicates the electrical damping of the driver. Q_{ES} depends on both the driver's internal DC resistance (R_E) and the driver's ability to act as an internal voltage generator. Recall from Chapter 1 that a driver's moving voice coil generates a "counter" voltage (back EMF) which acts as an opposition to the current from the amplifier. When both voice coils are used, whether connected in parallel or in series, Q_{ES} is always cut in half. This change in Q_{ES} affects how the driver can best be used. For example, since EBP depends on the value of Q_{ES}, sometimes a dual-voice-coil driver can work better in a closed box or, using two separate voice coils, it can be better suited to a vented box. An 8" dual-voice-coil subwoofer is such the case. For this driver, *Table 4-3* shows an EBP = 32 when one voice coil is used as opposed to an EBP = 64 when both are used.

Another effect of using both voice coils connected in parallel is an increase in the driver's voltage sensitivity. For example, *Table 4-3* indicates that the 8" dual-voice-coil woofer goes from a sensitivity of 88.6 dB, when only one voice coil is used, to 94.1 dB when both voice coils are connected in parallel. *Table 6-2* shows identical dual-voice-coil woofers in various combinations, and compares the pa-

Table 6-2. Comparison of Various Interconnections of Dual-Voice-Coil Subwoofers

System B	System 1B	System 2B	System 3B[2]	System 4B[3]

System B	System 1B	System 2B	System 3B[2]	System 4B[3]
Dual-voice-coil driver. One voice coil is connected to one channel of a stereo amplifier.	Dual-voice-coil driver. The two voice coils are connected in series and go to one channel of a stereo amplifier.	Two identical dual-voice-coil drivers. A voice coil in each driver is connected in series with a voice coil in the other driver. Each pair in series goes to a separate channel of the stereo amplifier.	Dual-voice-coil driver. Both voice coils are connected in parallel and go to one channel of a stereo amplifier.	Two identical dual-voice-coil drivers. A voice coil in each driver is connected in parallel to a voice coil in the other driver. Each paralleled pair goes to a separate channel of the stereo amplifier.
Single Driver B	As compared to B	As compared to B	As compared to B	As compared to B
F_S	F_S	F_S	F_S	F_S
Q_{ES}	$\frac{1}{2}(Q_{ES})$	$\frac{1}{2}(Q_{ES})$	$\frac{1}{2}(Q_{ES})$	$\frac{1}{2}(Q_{ES})$
Q_{MS}	Q_{MS}	Q_{MS}	Q_{MS}	Q_{MS}
Q_{TS}	$Q'_{TS} < Q_{TS}{}^1$	$Q'_{TS} < Q_{TS}{}^1$	$Q'_{TS} < Q_{TS}{}^1$	$Q'_{TS} < Q_{TS}{}^1$
V_{AS}	V_{AS}	$2(V_{AS})$	V_{AS}	$2(V_{AS})$
(R_E)	$2(R_E)$	$2(R_E)$	$\frac{1}{2}(R_E)$	$\frac{1}{2}(R_E)$
S_D (piston area)	S_D	$2(S_D)$	S_D	$2(S_D)$
X_{MAX}	X_{MAX}	X_{MAX}	X_{MAX}	X_{MAX}
SPL – dB/2.83V/1m	SPL – dB/2.83V/1m	SPL – +6 dB/2.83V/1m	SPL – +6 dB/2.83V/1m	SPL – +12 dB/2.83V/1m
P_E (power limit)	P_E (power limit)	$2(P_E)$	P_E (power limit)	$2(P_E)$
L_{VC} (voice coil inductance)	$2(L_{VC})$	$2(L_{VC})$	$\frac{1}{2}(L_{VC})$	$\frac{1}{2}(L_{VC})$

Notes:

1.
$$Q'_{TS} = \frac{Q_{ES}Q_{MS}}{Q_{ES} + 2Q_{MS}}$$

2. Excellent choice for increasing sensitivity by 6 dB and yet only using one driver.

3. Good choice for bandpass subwoofer +12 dB increase in sensitivity, *careful,* impedance cut in half.

rameters of each combination to that of a single dual-voice-coil woofer using only one voice coil (of single-driver System B). In *Table 4-3*, two separate types of measurements were taken on a dual-voice-coil woofer. In the first case, only a single voice coil was connected to the test equipment, and the measurements are given on the "single voice coil" line in *Table 4-3*. They are the base values for the "System B" in *Table 6-2*. In the second case, the measurements were made with both "voice coils in parallel," given on a line indicated as such in *Table 4-3*. The voltage sensitivities given in *Table 6-2* apply in most situations, and provide useful comparisons to single-driver System B; however, the sensitivities indicated should not be taken as absolutes.

A Dual-Voice-Coil Subwoofer Example

Let's use a 12" dual-voice-coil woofer in a design example. *Table 4-3* indicates that this driver will have a voltage sensitivity of 96 dB/2.83V/1m when both voice coils are connected in parallel. *Figure 6-5* shows the correct values, from *Table 4-3* for a 12" woofer with the dual-voice-coils connected in parallel, entered into the **DRIVER SPECIFICATION** window of TOP BOX. *Table 4-3* further tells us that the EBP = 36.6 when both voice coils are connected in parallel, meaning that a closed box will have the best results. The **BOX DESIGN** window of TOP BOX indicates the box volume as 775 liters for a maximally flat response; however, a much smaller box of 175 liters was selected for the design.

Entering 175 liters (6.18 ft^3) into the **BOX DESIGN** window, TOP BOX informs us that this box size will have F_3 = 29.1 Hz, Q_{TC} = 1.09, and a response peak = 1.75 dB. The **BOX DESIGN** window predicts that the voltage sensitivity of the system will be 96 dB, just as indicated in *Table 4-3*, which is 5.3 dB more than the 90.7 dB indicated when this 12" woofer is used with only one voice coil connected. *Figure 6-6* shows the frequency response of this system, indicating a 1.75 dB peak between 40 Hz and 60 Hz. The crosshairs indicate that the -3 dB point on the response curve will take place at 29.2 Hz. We shall use this subwoofer in Chapter 8 and match it with a pair of bass-shy small satellite speakers like the system shown in *Figure 6-4*. Both channels of the stereo amplifier will go to the dual-voice-coil subwoofer, which uses an 8-way speaker terminal for the four lines coming in and the four lines going out to the satellites. A crossover is needed to separate the frequencies which go to the dual-voice-coil subwoofer from the higher frequencies going out to the pair of satellite speakers.

THE BANDPASS SUBWOOFER

An unusual subwoofer design is the bandpass subwoofer. It uses a unique enclosure which eliminates the need for a crossover. All one sees on the outside is a port from which the sound emanates. The driver is hidden completely inside the box. "Bandpass" is used in its name because the enclosure itself acts like a crossover, so the subwoofer passes only a limited range of frequencies into the outside air. For example, a bandpass subwoofer may allow only the group of frequencies between 30 Hz and 90 Hz to pass into a room. Inside the bandpass subwoofer, an interior partition separates the two chambers. The woofer(s) are mounted on this inner partition. One chamber formed by the partition is totally sealed while the other is

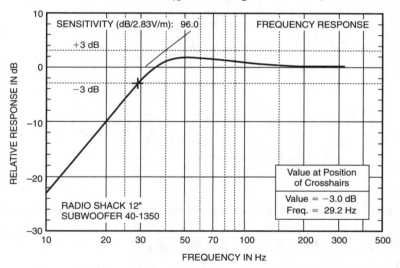

TOP BOX

DRIVER SPECIFICATION

RESONANT FREQUENCY (Fs)	21
ELECTRICAL Q (Qe)	.582
MECHANICAL Q (Qm)	4.58
EQUIV. VOL. (Vas) liters	497
D.C. RESISTANCE (Re)	1.89
COIL INDUCTANCE (Lvc) mh	.402
POWER RATING watts	60
PEAK THROW mm	11.7
PISTON AREA (Sd) sq cm	532

BOX DESIGN

Box Vol(Q= .71), liters	775
Optimum 3 dB Freq, Hz	25.0
Box Volume (Vb) liters	175
3 dB Frequency (F3) Hz	29.1
Closed Box Q	1.09
Sensitivity (2.83 V) dB	96.0
Reponse Peak, dB	1.75

COMMAND

Write to Printer (Y/N) ? n

MESSAGES

Closed Box Configuration

Ctrl-H for HELP

Figure 6-5. Closed Box Design with $Q_{TC} = 0.71$ (maximally flat and $V_B = 775$ liters) and $Q_{TC} = 1.09$ ($V_B = 175$ liters)

SENSITIVITY (dB/2.83V/m): 96.0

FREQUENCY RESPONSE

+3 dB

−3 dB

RADIO SHACK 12″
SUBWOOFER 40-1350

Value at Position
of Crosshairs

Value = −3.0 dB
Freq. = 29.2 Hz

FREQUENCY IN Hz

Figure 6-6. Closed Box Using 12″ Dual-Voice-Coil Subwoofer with 175-liter (6.18 ft³) Box Size (Generated Using TOP BOX)

vented to the outside air. *Figure 6-7* illustrates such a bandpass subwoofer which uses two woofers, mounted on the same partition, with one driver reversed and wired out of phase to take advantage of the push-pull mode.

Even though a patent was issued for a "passband" in the 1950s, it was not until the British company, KEF, issued its model 104-2 speaker under engineer Laurie Fincham that commercial companies took notice of this method of driver loading. In 1991, Dr. Joe D'Appolito presented his paper, "Designing Symmetric Response Bandpass Enclosures," to the 91st Audio Engineering Society. His ideas are incorporated into TOP BOX, which can design fourth-order and sixth-order bandpass subwoofers. A fourth-order bandpass subwoofer has *both an upper and a lower* F_3 (the point where response is -3dB below the reference level), called F_U and F_L, respectively. Below F_L and above F_U, the response of the bandpass subwoofer drops off at the rate of 12 dB/octave. If one chooses to use a sixth-order bandpass subwoofer, TOP BOX will calculate a specific inductor (L_E) and capacitor (C_E) to be placed in series between the amplifier and the subwoofer. The rate of drop in response outside of the band of passed frequencies in the sixth-order bandpass subwoofer is 18 dB/octave.

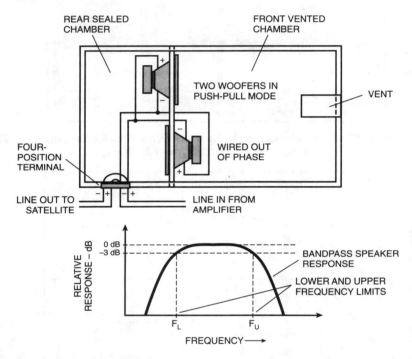

Figure 6-7. Bandpass Subwoofer Using Two Drivers in Push-Pull Mode

DESIGNING AN INTEGRATED BANDPASS SUBWOOFER-SATELLITE SYSTEM

Let us examine an 8" dual-voice-coil woofer as a prospect for a bandpass subwoofer system. As noted earlier, this driver has an EBP of 32 if a single voice coil is used, and an EBP of 64 if both voice coils are connected in parallel. This occurs because QES is cut in half in the latter case, which makes it a good choice for a vented enclosure such as the bandpass subwoofer.

When matching a subwoofer to satellite speakers, you must be concerned with comparing the sensitivity of one to the other. Suppose we have designed a satellite system with a sensitivity of 98.4 dB/2.83V/1m. Using only one of the dual voice coils, the sensitivity of an 8" dual-voice-coil driver is 88.6 dB/2.83V/1m. This would not provide an even match for our designed satellite system. Looking at system 4B of *Table 6-2,* which uses two 8″ dual-voice-coil drivers with voice coils wired in parallel, we see that the voltage sensitivity increases by +12 dB over that of a system using a single driver (System B). Adding 12 dB to 88.6 dB, we get 100.6 dB, giving us a sensitivity closer to that which is needed. Again, we select the fourth-order bandpass design option in TOP BOX. We need parameters to enter into the **DRIVER SPECIFICATION** window.

The parameters for the 8″ dual-voice-coil woofer in *Table 4-3* using a single voice coil must be converted to new values using the changes indicated in *Table 6-2* for System 4B.

Table 6-3. Converted System 4B Parameters

8″ Subwoofer	Single Voice Coil	Per Table 6-2	New System 4B
F_S (Hz)	51	same	51
Q_{ES}	1.59	½ (Q_{ES})	0.795
Q_{MS}	2.78	same	2.78
V_{AS} (l)	40.47	2 (V_{AS})	81
R_E (Ω)	5.07	½ (R_E)	2.53
L_{VC} (mH)	0.657	½ (L_{VC})	0.328
P_E (W)	50	2 (P_E)	100
X_{MAX} (mm)	7.87	same	7.87
S_D (cm²)	214	2 (S_D)	428

The parameter values for system 4B entered into TOP BOX's **DRIVER SPECIFICA-TION** window are shown in *Figure 6-8*.

Next TOP BOX asks in the **BOX DESIGN** window for the upper and lower frequency cut-off points, F_U and F_L. After trying several possible values, the best compromise develops, as shown in *Figure 6-8,* when we use F_U = 115 Hz and F_L = 45 Hz. The combination of smaller box size, a reasonable lower F_L and an upper F_U that can be made to work with the satellite speakers is the result. Taking the air load on the drivers into account, TOP BOX predicts a sensitivity of 98.9 dB/2.83V/1m, a good match to the satellites. We ask for a port length using two 4″ diameter tubes and TOP BOX responds that each should be 5.27 cm (2⁵/₆₄″). TOP BOX tells us that V_f, the front volume where the vents are located, should be 53.1 liters, and that V_b, the back volume or sealed chamber, should be 54.4 liters. For proper operation, the sealed chamber should not have any air leak to the vented chamber.

Remember that TOP BOX can overlay two design responses. This capability can be used to integrate better the subwoofer design and the satellite speaker design. Either design can be called up on TOP BOX and tweaked to arrive at the desired response. By saving the frequency response graph of the previous bandpass design, the frequency response of the satellite system can be overlain on the bandpass system, as shown in *Figure 6-9*. In *Figure 6-9,* the two frequency response graphs coincide at 112.4 Hz, each −2.6 dB down from the reference level.

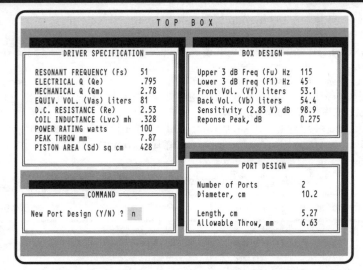

Figure 6-8. Bandpass Subwoofer Design Using 8″ Dual-Voice-Coil Woofer with Voice Coils in Parallel (F_L = 45 Hz and F_U = 115 Hz)

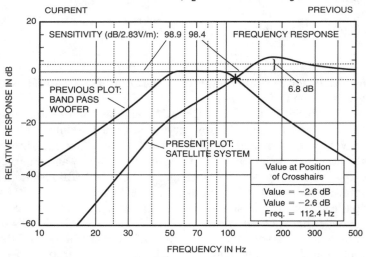

Figure 6-9. Overlay of TOP BOX Frequency Response for Bandpass Subwoofer and Satellite System (Generated Using TOP BOX)

SUMMARY

The 6.8 dB peak in the satellite system response of *Figure 6-9* in the 175-Hz region may serve a purpose. As mentioned in Chapter 1 and discussed further in the next chapter, speakers which are free standing in a room will experience a loss in low frequencies as a consequence of diffraction. This loss progresses up to 6 dB as it reaches into the deeper bass, which can bring the peak predicted for the satellites down considerably. In the next chapter, crossover design will be used as a technique to arrange two drivers into forming a flatter response, particularly when taking into account considerations such as diffraction loss.

Crossovers

7

THE CROSSOVER CIRCUIT

The crossover is a key element in the overall multiple-driver speaker system design. Learning to do the crossover design to match the drivers selected will give you a much better speaker system in the end. Taking a "ready-made" crossover from a store shelf is similar to buying a "one-size-fits-all" pair of shoes and trying to wear them for all occasions.

2-WAY CROSSOVERS

In a 2-way speaker system, high frequencies should go to the tweeter and low frequencies to the woofer. A 2-way crossover, which uses inductors and capacitors, can accomplish this by acting as an electrical filter. As we saw in Chapter 1, an inductor presents an ever increasing opposition to current in an AC circuit as frequencies get higher. The opposition to current of an inductor in an AC circuit is called *inductive reactance,* symbolized as X_L and measured in ohms, just like resistance. Using the formula $X_L = 2\pi FL$, and keeping the inductor value (L) constant, we can see that the variable inductive reactance, X_L, increases as F increases. Thus, if you place an inductor in series with a woofer and apply an AC signal, higher frequencies will be increasingly attenuated or "rolled off" from the woofer's response. The high-frequency attenuation is a direct result of the increasing opposition (inductive reactance) of the inductor. A capacitor will do exactly the reverse: when it is placed in series with a tweeter, it will increasingly attenuate low frequencies attempting to get through to the tweeter.

Figure 7-1a shows the responses of a woofer and a tweeter resulting from three different types of 2-way crossovers. Let us trace the path of the dotted-solid curve, which shows the effects of using a 1st-order crossover in a 2-way speaker system. As we go from left to right, we see the woofer's response begins to roll off at 200 Hz. At 825 Hz, the responses of both the woofer and the tweeter are attenuated -3 dB below the reference response of 0 dB. However, after 825 Hz, the response of the tweeter increases to 0 dB while the response of the woofer continually rolls off. The intersection of the woofer and tweeter response curves occurs at the *crossover frequency,* represented by F_C. Frequencies above F_C will increasingly follow the low opposition path to the tweeter rather than the higher opposition path which leads to the woofer. You must choose F_C wisely, carefully weighing certain characteristics of both drivers to avoid further difficulties, as we shall soon see.

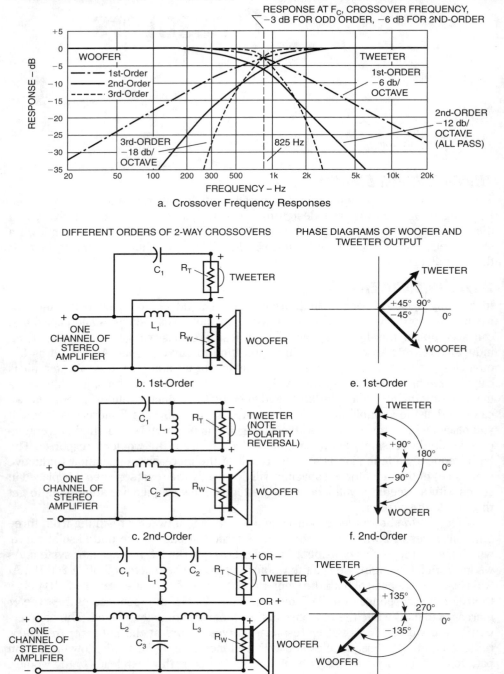

RESPONSE AT F_C, CROSSOVER FREQUENCY, −3 dB FOR ODD ORDER, −6 dB FOR 2ND-ORDER

a. Crossover Frequency Responses

DIFFERENT ORDERS OF 2-WAY CROSSOVERS

PHASE DIAGRAMS OF WOOFER AND TWEETER OUTPUT

b. 1st-Order

e. 1st-Order

c. 2nd-Order

f. 2nd-Order

d. 3rd-Order

g. 3rd-Order

Figure 7-1. Different Order Crossover Responses, Circuits and Phase Diagrams

Figures 7-1b, 7-1c and *7-1d* show different orders of 2-way crossovers. Notice in *Figure 7-1b,* that each parallel branch of the crossover has 1 component, categorizing it as a 1st-order crossover. In *Figure 7-1c,* each branch has 2 components, making it a 2nd-order crossover. In *Figure 7-1d,* 3 components per branch define it as a 3rd-order crossover. The effect of increasing the number of components in a crossover is clearly shown in the curves of *Figure 7-1a.* As each crossover increases to a higher order, the rate of attenuation (slope) of each response curve increases. Higher-order crossovers are sharper filtering devices. As shown in *Figure 7-1a,* 1st-order crossovers attenuate at the rate of -6 dB/octave, 2nd-order at -12 dB/octave and 3rd-order at -18 dB/octave. To understand what this means, look at the vertical line coming up from 300 Hz as it intersects the three different tweeter response curves. On the dotted curve (3rd-order), the response is attenuated (down) -27 dB from the reference response (0 dB); on the solid curve (2nd-order) it is -16 dB down; but on the dotted-solid curve (1st-order) it is only -8 dB down. This shows that if you choose a low F_C (such as 825 Hz) and use a 1st-order crossover, a substantial amount of higher bass frequencies will get through to the tweeter. This can easily result in tweeter damage that could be avoided by using a higher-order crossover. A different set of equations is used to calculate the inductor and capacitor values for each order of crossover.

Figures 7-1e, 7-1f and *7-1g* show phase diagrams using vectors to represent the output of the tweeter and woofer. The output is affected in each case by the order of the crossover. A 2-way system which employs a 1st-order crossover will have the tweeter output rotated by $+45°$ and a woofer output rotated by $-45°$. At F_C, the 90° phase difference between the two driver outputs will add up to produce a final response at the 0 dB line. Therefore, what seems to be a hole or "dip" in the response at F_C in *Figure 7-1a* actually will be a straight line in a properly designed system. In each successive diagram, every time a component is added to each branch of the crossover, the tweeter output rotates by an additional $+45°$ while the woofer output changes by another $-45°$. This leads to a total phase difference of 180° when using a 2nd-order crossover, and to a 270° phase difference when using the 3rd-order crossover. Notice that the polarity of the tweeter is reversed in the 2nd-order crossover, *Figure 7-1c.* As we shall soon see in the section on 2nd-order crossovers, this has a great deal to do with phase.

C and L for 1st-Order 2-Way Crossover

A 1st-order crossover response is -3 dB down at F_C, when $R_T = X_C$ and $R_W = X_L$. We can substitute these values into the X_C and X_L equations and solve for C and L as follows:

$$R_T = \frac{1}{2\pi F_C C} \qquad R_W = 2\pi F_C L$$

Where:
R_T = tweeter's rated impedance in **ohms**
C = crossover series capacitor in **farads**

$$C = \frac{1}{6.28318 F_C R_T} \qquad L = \frac{R_W}{6.28318 F_C}$$

F_C = crossover frequency in **Hz**
R_W = woofer's rated impedance in **ohms**
L = crossover series inductor in **henries**

$$C = \frac{0.159155}{F_C R_T} \qquad L = \frac{0.159155 R_W}{F_C}$$

$2\pi = 6.28318$

Since the capacitance is usually in microfarads and the inductance is usually in millihenries, the equations for C and L are converted to:

$$C \text{ (in } \mu F) = \frac{159,155}{F_C R_T} \quad \text{and} \quad L \text{ (in mH)} = \frac{159.155 \, R_W}{F_C}$$

GENERAL REQUIREMENTS FOR CROSSOVER DESIGN

In a 2-way crossover design, the first design consideration is the choice of a tweeter to accompany the woofer. Many people think that driver sensitivities must match exactly, but this is not necessarily the case. First, by using resistors, the sensitivity of a tweeter can be brought down several dB to match the sensitivity of the woofer. Second, it may be desirable for the woofer to be more efficient than the tweeter because of diffraction losses which, as frequencies decrease, will progressively reduce low-frequency sound pressure levels down by -6 dB *if* speakers are placed on stands that are set well into the room.

Third, as a criteria for selecting a crossover frequency, be sure that the frequency response of each driver *overlaps* and remains flat on either side of the crossover frequency for a reasonable frequency spread. Try to select a crossover frequency at least *one octave* away from the driver's resonant frequency. This is particularly true of tweeters, which can give quite a harsh sound if frequencies near the tweeter's F_S are allowed to be reproduced. These choices, geared toward your particular drivers, provide a good start towards producing a first quality crossover. "Off-the-shelf" crossovers have arbitrary crossover frequencies, with no concern for driver F_S nor the region where the drivers' responses overlap.

ACTUAL 1st-ORDER 2-WAY CROSSOVER DESIGN

You have a tweeter with an $F_S = 967$ Hz and with a response that goes down to 1750 Hz before dropping off. You wish to use this tweeter with a 6½" woofer which has a similar sensitivity and a frequency response which stays relatively flat to 4250 Hz before rolling off. Since a 1st-order filter rolls off slowly at the rate of 6 dB/octave *(Figure 7-1a)* as frequency varies, it would be wise to position the F_C on the frequency axis as far away from the tweeter F_S as is reasonable and yet not approach the edge where the woofer's response falls off. One octave higher than the tweeter's F_S is 1934 Hz; two octaves is 3868 Hz. A crossover frequency of 3500 Hz would be suitable in this case. If the nominal impedance of both tweeter and woofer is 8 ohms then, in order to find the inductor and capacitor, we would substitute $F_C = 3500$ Hz, $R_T = 8$ ohms and $R_W = 8$ ohms into the previous 1st-order equations to find L and C, as follows:

$$L = \frac{159.155 \times 8}{3500} = 0.3646 = 0.36 \text{ mH (rounded to the nearest hundredth)}$$

$$C = \frac{159,155}{3500 \times 8} = 5.684 = 5.7 \, \mu F \text{ (rounded to the nearest tenth)}$$

However, before you go to a store to purchase these components, there are some difficulties with the 1st-order crossover that would be wise to consider.

IMPROVING THE DESIGN

Refer again to *Figure 7-1a*. The primary deficiency of the 1st-order crossover is that, despite the capacitor, a significant amount of low-frequency response *still* gets through to the tweeter. The best way to alleviate this shortcoming would be to increase the *sharpness* of the crossover's filtering action. The 2nd-order crossover shown does just that. However, there is a price to pay. Look at *Figure 7-1c*. Notice that an inductor and capacitor have been *added* to the circuit and that the polarity $(+/-)$ of the tweeter has been *reversed*.

The additional inductor and capacitor wired in parallel with the driver provide a *path of least resistance* for undesirable frequencies that manage to pass through the first barrier, producing a crossover with increased filtering abilities; therefore, the greater attenuation of the tweeter response before the crossover frequency, and the greater attenuation of the woofer response after the crossover frequency. Where the 1st-order crossover curves meet at the -3 dB point at the crossover frequency, the 2nd-order crossover curves meet at the -6 dB point. Recall that the 2nd-order crossover response curves fall at a rate of -12 dB/octave away from F_C. The 2nd-order crossover is considered to be the minimum filtering action sufficient to prevent bass frequencies from reaching tweeters. In general, a 2nd-order crossover is not as sensitive to the spacing of drivers as is a 1st-order crossover. In any case, it is best to keep the driver spacing close and the driver's centers in a vertical alignment.

In the 1st-order crossover, the response of the tweeter is *90° out of phase* from the response of the woofer at F_C. As shown in *Figure 7-1f*, in the 2nd-order crossover, the normal tweeter response is *180° out of phase* from the woofer response at F_C. Unless we do something, a large dip in the response at F_C will occur. By reversing the polarity of the tweeter in the 2nd-order crossover, the responses of the two drivers are put *back in phase* at the crossover frequency. Since two drivers driven in parallel from the same source have a $+6$ dB greater sensitivity then, by meeting at a point -6 dB below reference level, the two driver responses *sum to unity* at the crossover frequency (i.e., produce a flat response at the reference level). Recall, in the 1st-order crossover it was -3 dB.

C and L for a 2nd-Order 2-Way Crossover

Second-order crossovers are in the class of *even-order networks*. Even-order networks are further divided into two categories. The category that can pass all frequencies with the same amplitude as the original (but shift the phase) is called "All-Pass" or "Linkwitz-Riley." In the 1970s, Siegfried Linkwitz[1] discovered that the All-Pass type of crossover will produce a symmetrical acoustical radiation pattern which has a lobe of maximum sound pressure on a central axis *perpendicular* to the speaker. This type of radiation pattern is considered better for home high-fidelity listening. The second even-order category, which produces a better off-axis response pattern, is an older type known as a "Constant-Power" crossover. This type of crossover is considered by many as more appropriate for sound reinforcement systems where listening will be done off-axis in a large reverberant field such as an auditorium. Odd-order 2-way networks are categorized as *both* All-Pass and Constant-Power simultaneously.

The following equations are for a 2nd-order, All-Pass, 2-way crossover. The constants are converted to give answers in microfarads and millihenries.

[1] S. Linkwitz, "Passive Crossover Networks for Noncoincident Drivers," *JAES*, March 1978.

Tweeter Section	Woofer Section
$C_1 = \dfrac{1}{4\pi F_C R_T} \times 10^6 = \dfrac{79{,}577}{F_C R_T}$ (in µF)	$C_2 = \dfrac{1}{4\pi F_C R_W} \times 10^6 = \dfrac{79{,}577}{F_C R_W}$ (in µF)
$L_1 = \dfrac{R_T}{\pi F_C} \times 10^3 = \dfrac{318.3 \times R_T}{F_C}$ (in mH)	$L_2 = \dfrac{R_W}{\pi F_C} \times 10^3 = \dfrac{318.3 \times R_W}{F_C}$ (in mH)

Where:
R_T = tweeter rated impedance in **ohms**
C_1 = tweeter section capacitor in **µF**
L_1 = tweeter section inductor in **mH**
F_C = crossover frequency in **Hz**

R_W = woofer rated impedance in **ohms**
C_2 = woofer section capacitor in **µF**
L_2 = woofer section inductor in **mH**
π = 3.14159

Actual 2nd-Order Design

We will use the same tweeter and woofer drivers and the same crossover frequency of 3500 Hz as for the 1st-order crossover to design a 2nd-order 2-way crossover. R_T = 8 ohms and R_W = 8 ohms. The values for C_1, L_1, C_2 and L_2 (to the nearest hundredth) are:

$$C_1 = \frac{79{,}577}{3500 \times 8} = 2.84 \text{ µF} \qquad C_2 = \frac{79{,}577}{3500 \times 8} = 2.84 \text{ µF}$$

$$L_1 = \frac{318.3 \times 8}{3500} = 0.73 \text{ mH} \qquad L_2 = \frac{318.3 \times 8}{3500} = 0.73 \text{ mH}$$

Testing the frequency response of your completed speaker as shown in Chapter 2, particularly in the region bordering the crossover frequency, is highly recommended.

FURTHER IMPROVEMENT TO THE CROSSOVER NETWORK

In the equations used to calculate L and C values, both the rated impedance of the tweeter and woofer, R_T and R_W, have been considered as resistances. For best design results, the crossover wants to see these as resistances, not just at the crossover frequency, F_C, but also for frequencies a considerable distance before and after F_C. As we have seen, our voice coil drivers behave nothing like resistors. By using an *impedance compensation* network (sometimes called a conjugate network), consisting of a resistor and a capacitor, usually used in the woofer section of a 2-way crossover, the driver's impedance curve can be made flat. This is shown in *Figure 7-2a*. The solid line is the impedance curve prior to impedance compensation, whereas the dotted line shows the results after compensation. As shown in *Figure 7-2b*, the impedance compensation network is connected in the woofer circuit after the crossover and before the driver.

The following equations are used to calculate the value of the capacitor, C, and the resistor, R_C, shown in the impedance compensation network of *Figure 7-2b*.

$$R_C = 1.25 \times R_E \text{ ohms}$$

$$C = \frac{10^3 \times L_{VC}}{R_C{}^2} \text{ µF}$$

Where:
R_E is the voice coil DC resistance in **ohms**
L_{VC} is the voice coil inductance in **mH**

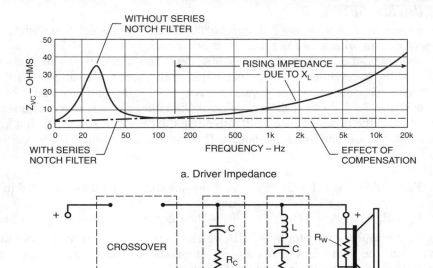

a. Driver Impedance

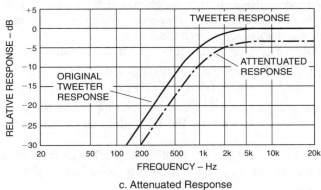

b. Impedance Compensation and Notch Filter Networks

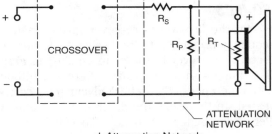

c. Attenuated Response

d. Attenuation Network

Figure 7-2. Notch Filter, Impedance Compensation and Attenuation Networks

ATTENUATION NETWORK

You have a woofer with a voltage sensitivity of 89 dB/2.83V/m which you wish to use in a 2-way design with a tweeter whose rated sensitivity is 94 dB/2.83V/m. The tweeter will sound too bright in this speaker system. You would like to decrease the sensitivity of the tweeter somewhat to match the woofer better. We can attenuate the *entire* tweeter response curve, as shown in *Figure 7-2c,* using only two resistors. As shown in *Figure 7-2d,* these resistors are positioned after the crossover. The series resistor, R_S, and the parallel resistor, R_P, attenuate the tweeter's sensitivity, but keep the rated resistance of the tweeter constant. The equations to evaluate these resistors are:

$$R_P = 10^{A/20} \times R_T/(1 - 10^{A/20})$$

$$R_S = R_T - (1/R_P + 1/R_T)^{-1}$$

where:

A = the amount of attenuation needed in **negative dB**

R_T = the rated tweeter impedance in **ohms**

Let us attenuate the tweeter by −5 dB, which will bring the sensitivity down to 89 dB/2.83V/1m, the same as the woofer. To attenuate an 8-ohm tweeter by 5 dB, substitute A = −5 dB and R_T = 8 into the first equation.

$$R_P = 10^{-5/20} \times 8/(1 - 10^{-5/20}) = 10^{-0.25} \times 8/(1 - 10^{-0.25})$$
$$= 0.5623 \times 8/(1 - 0.5623) = 10.28 \text{ ohms}$$

Using a scientific calculator, it is easy to find $10^{-5/20}$. First, we know that the exponent −5/20 = −1/4 = −0.25. Using the calculator, enter **10**, press the $\mathbf{Y^X}$ button, enter **0.25**, press the ± button (to change 0.25 to −0.25), press = and we get 0.5623, which is 10 raised to the −0.25 power. With the exponent evaluated, we substitute that value and solve for R_P = 10.28 ohms.

Now that we know R_P, we substitute this value in the second equation to find R_S.

$$R_S = 8 - (1/10.28 + 1/8)^{-1} = 8 - (0.0973 + 0.125)^{-1}$$
$$= 8 - (0.2223)^{-1} = 8 - 4.498 = 3.5 \text{ ohms}$$

The solution is straightforward. Recall that raising a quantity to the −1 power means to *take the reciprocal* and we use the 1/X button on the scientific calculator to do that.

Using the two resistors in the attenuation network shown in *Figure 7-2d,* the tweeter response curve can be lowered from the solid line to the dotted line, as shown in *Figure 7-2c.*

3rd-ORDER CROSSOVERS

As shown in *Figure 7-1a,* the 3rd-order crossover gives greater attenuation and, hence, greater low-frequency protection to the tweeter. The phase difference of the two sections of a 3rd-order crossover is shown to be 270° in *Figure 7-1g.* The two outputs sum much like those with a 90° phase difference. Although many people claim they cannot hear a difference, a theoretical advantage occurs when the polarity of the tweeter is reversed. In this case, the difference in the arrival times of both outputs is made smaller, giving better "group delay" performance.

The 3rd-order Butterworth crossover is both All-Pass and Constant-Power and has the ability to filter at the rate of 18 dB/octave. The crossover is shown in *Figure 7-1d* and the response in *Figure 7-1a*. The equations to calculate the capacitor values in microfarads and inductor values in millihenries are as follows:

Tweeter Section

$$C_1 \text{ (in } \mu F) = \frac{106,103}{F_C R_T}$$

$$C_2 \text{ (in } \mu F) = \frac{318,391}{F_C R_T}$$

$$L_1 \text{ (in mH)} = \frac{119.37 \times R_T}{F_C}$$

Woofer Section

$$L_2 \text{ (in mH)} = \frac{238.73 \times R_W}{F_C}$$

$$L_3 \text{ (in mH)} = \frac{79.58 \times R_W}{F_C}$$

$$C_3 \text{ (in } \mu F) = \frac{212,207}{F_C R_W}$$

As a speaker designer, be aware that using a 3rd-order crossover does not automatically ensure that the actual acoustic roll-off attenuation of a specific driver will be -18 dB/octave. Each driver has its own natural roll-off and this, combined with the crossover's electrical filtering rate, gives the actual acoustic roll-off. For example, if you have a woofer whose natural roll-off is -12 dB/octave, then there is a good chance that using a 1st-order crossover's electrical -6 dB/octave filtering rate will produce an actual acoustic roll-off of -18 dB/octave. You are advised to read the discussions on the designs of Chapter 8 to help improve your intuition of when to use a certain order crossover with a certain driver to achieve a desired actual acoustic roll-off rate.

CROSSOVER EFFECT ON ACOUSTICAL PATTERN

Beside filter sharpness, one of the main differences between the 3rd-order crossover and the 2nd-order All-Pass crossover, is the acoustical radiation patterns they produce. *Figure 7-3* compares a typical vertical response radiation pattern of a speaker system using a 3rd-order crossover with a speaker system using a 2nd-order crossover, both at approximately 3000 Hz. The listener (L) is located on the 0° axis relative to the speaker. The diagram illustrates "lobing" behavior, in which locations of low-intensity sound pressures are created alongside lobes of high intensity. As the frequency being emitted drops, the lobes become wider. If you raised your body from sitting position to standing position, you would find that the sound intensities of the higher frequencies would vary at different heights. At certain places the speaker may sound duller, at other places brighter. These radiation patterns are dependent on the crossover order and the spacing of the drivers. The main difference between the vertical radiation patterns of a 3rd-order crossover and the 2nd-order all-pass crossover is that the radiation pattern of the 3rd-order crossover is tilted, whereas the radiation pattern of the 2nd-order crossover is symmetric with respect to the 0° axis. These differences imply that in some cases tilting speakers up may work best while, in other situations, facing them directly toward the listener might produce optimum results. Since acoustic radiation patterns affect the overall sound of a speaker, speaker builders have hoped for a way to control this aspect of the design. Recently, an exceptional speaker design that consistently produces symmetrical radiation patterns has been discovered. Let us take a look at the unique architecture of this design.

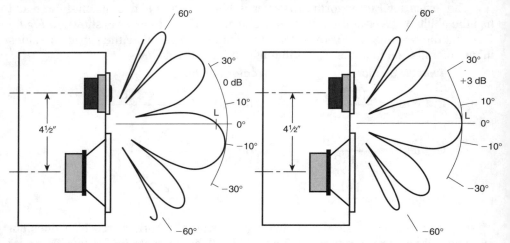

a. 2-Way Speaker System 3rd-Order Crossover at 3000 hertz. Driver Spacing 4.5 Inches

b. 2-Way Speaker System 2nd-Order Crossover at 3000 hertz. Driver Spacing 4.5 Inches

Figure 7-3. Acoustical Radiation Patterns Using Different Crossovers

THE D'APPOLITO 3/2 SPEAKER GEOMETRY

In his 1983 paper, "A Geometric Approach to Eliminating Lobing Errors in Multiway Loudspeakers," Dr. Joseph D'Appolito found a way to create a symmetric vertical radiation pattern from speakers. Reading the work of Linkwitz, it occurred to him that a *symmetrical* positioning of 3 drivers in a 2-way design, used with a 3rd-order crossover, would produce the *quasi-spherical* vertical response pattern illustrated by the *solid curved line* (A) in *Figure 7-4*. He found that, in order for the 3/2 geometry to work properly, the distance between the centers of the adjacent drivers should be kept close to one wavelength of the crossover's frequency, F_C. If you wish to calculate this distance in inches, divide the speed of sound (13,503.94 inches/second) by the crossover frequency, F_C. The elegance of the 3/2 driver arrangement is that some type of symmetrical vertical radiation pattern is produced *no matter* what crossover type is used.

Figure 7-4 shows two other symmetrical radiation patterns that can be produced using the D'Appolito 3/2 driver geometry. A 2nd-order All-Pass (Linkwitz-Riley) crossover produces the large symmetric lobe shown as the *slotted curved line* (B). This type of radiation pattern is useful if you want your speaker to produce very little sound pressure in the off-axis regions, so that reflections from nearby walls and floors are greatly reduced. The *point/slotted curved line* (C) shows a symmetric radiation pattern that is produced when a *3rd-order* high-pass section of a crossover is combined with a *2nd-order* low-pass section. This shows that the 3/2 driver geometry produces a symmetric radiation pattern even when used with a *mixed-order* cross-over. It is of great benefit to speaker builders that the 3/2 geometry works with *odd-order* crossovers, *even-order* crossovers or *mixed-order* crossovers.

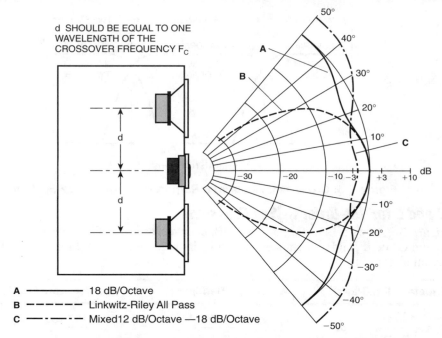

d SHOULD BE EQUAL TO ONE
WAVELENGTH OF THE
CROSSOVER FREQUENCY F$_C$

A ————————— 18 dB/Octave
B ————————— Linkwitz-Riley All Pass
C ——·——·—— Mixed12 dB/Octave —18 dB/Octave

Figure 7-4. D'Appolito 3/2 Speaker System Geometry

3-WAY CROSSOVERS

There are several reasons why you may wish to use three drivers in a speaker system. One reason is the appetite for a more powerful bass. If you wish to use only one woofer per speaker system, this requires considering the use of larger diameter woofers, since they move larger amounts of air. However, larger woofers have drawbacks; their frequency responses are usually rougher and always more directional in the upper frequency ranges than those of smaller woofers. With regard to selecting a crossover frequency, a maxim sometimes used is: "Use a woofer *only* up to a frequency which has a wavelength equal to the driver's effective piston diameter." For a 12-inch woofer, this would place the boundary near 1300 Hz. If you were to adhere to this rule and want to use a 12-inch woofer in a 2-way system, you would need to find a tweeter that could be crossed over at 1300 Hz, a rare bird indeed, since this is where a tweeters' F$_S$ is often located. The only other option is to add a midrange driver to cover the middle span of frequencies which neither woofer nor tweeter can comfortably serve. Once this path is taken, you are obliged to undertake the more difficult task of designing a 3-way crossover.

As shown in *Figure 7-5,* a 3-way crossover divides the signal from the amplifier into three different frequency bands: the *low-pass,* the *high-pass,* and the band between them called the *bandpass band.* The bandpass section, which is passed to the midrange driver, can be made from a combination of high-pass and low-pass components. In order to divide the original signal into three different bands, two crossover frequencies need to be specified. F$_{LC}$ refers to the low-frequency crossover point and F$_{HC}$ refers to the high-frequency crossover point.

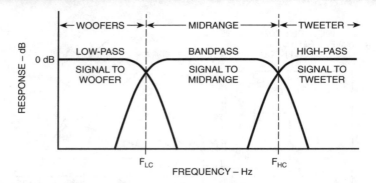

Figure 7-5. Crossover Response Required for the 3-Way System

C and L for 1st-Order 3-Way Crossover

Figure 7-6 shows a 1st-order, 3-way, 6 dB/octave crossover. The values of capacitors, C_1 and C_2, in μF, and inductances, L_1 and L_2, in mH, are calculated using the following equations:

Tweeter (High-Pass)	Midrange (Bandpass)	Woofer (Low-Pass)
$C_1 = \dfrac{159{,}155}{F_{HC}R_T}$ (in μF)	$C_2 = \dfrac{159{,}155}{F_{LC}R_M}$ (in μF)	$L_2 = \dfrac{159.155 \times R_W}{F_{LC}}$ (in mH)
	$L_1 = \dfrac{159.155 \times R_M}{F_{HC}}$ (in mH)	

Where:
C_1 = tweeter capacitor in μF
F_{HC} = high-frequency crossover in **Hz**
R_T = rated impedance of tweeter in **ohms**
L_1 = midrange inductor in **mH**
L_2 = woofer inductor in **mH**

R_M = rated impedance of midrange in o**hms**
C_2 = midrange capacitor in μF
F_{LC} = low-frequency crossover in **Hz**
R_W = rated impedance of woofer in **ohms**

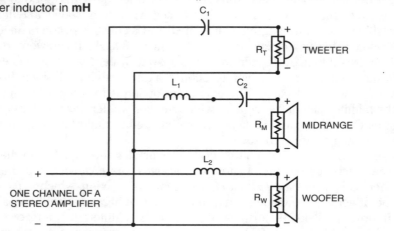

Figure 7-6. 1st-Order 3-Way 6 dB/Octave Crossover

The ideal would be for all three bands to fall into place as shown in *Figure 7-5*, combining to produce a flat frequency response. However, 3-way crossovers are not simple descendants of 2-way crossovers, but instead form a more difficult class of filters. In order to take a step closer to the ideal, one must face the fact that the reactances of the components of the midrange filter section interact with the reactances of the components of the tweeter and woofer filter sections. In order to compensate for this, the crossover frequencies F_{LC} and F_{HC} used in the equations of the midrange band must be brought closer together. We must replace F_{LC} and F_{HC} in the midrange band with two new frequencies, called F_{LC}' and F_{HC}', found using two special equations designed for this purpose.

How to Find F_{LC}' and F_{HC}'

The components of the bandpass band resonate at a central point between F_{LC} and F_{HC} which is found not by an *arithmetic* mean (i.e., a simple average), but instead by a *geometric* mean. The geometric mean, F_M, the central point at which resonance occurs, can be found using the equation:

$$F_M = \sqrt{F_{LC} \times F_{HC}}$$

It must also be true that the bandpass band will still resonate at F_M if we use F_{LC}' and F_{HC}'; therefore,

$$F_M = \sqrt{F_{LC}' \times F_{HC}'}$$

Since each expression is equal to F_M, they are equal to each other; therefore,

A $\quad F_{LC} \times F_{HC} = F_{LC}' \times F_{HC}'$

Next we need to know the *bandpass frequency ratio*, which is given by the fraction (F_{HC}/F_{LC}). If $F_{HC}/F_{LC} = 8$, this tells us that F_{HC} and F_{LC} are 3 octaves apart, since each octave involves a doubling of frequency and $2^3 = 8$. If we decrease the size of this ratio by one, we bring F_{HC} and F_{LC} closer together, giving us the ratio F_{HC}'/F_{LC}'. This ratio, F_{HC}'/F_{LC}', called the *design ratio*, is given by:

B $\quad F_{HC}'/F_{LC}' = (F_{HC}/F_{LC}) - 1$

Actual 1st-Order 3-Way Crossover Design

Let's apply the previous equations to design a simple 3-way 6 dB/octave crossover. First we will find the frequencies F_{HC}' and F_{LC}'. These values will be used in the equations for the crossover components forming the bandpass band. Our system uses a 4-ohm tweeter, an 8-ohm midrange, and an 8-ohm woofer crossed over at $F_{HC} = 4500$ Hz and $F_{LC} = 500$ Hz. Since $F_{HC}/F_{LC} = 4500/500 = 9$, the crossover frequencies are a little more than 3 octaves apart. Let's find the ratio F_{HC}'/F_{LC}' using Equation B.

$$F_{HC}'/F_{LC}' = (F_{HC}/F_{LC}) - 1 = 9 - 1 = 8$$

Therefore, multiplying both sides by F_{LC}':

$$F_{HC}' = 8F_{LC}'$$

Now we can find F_{LC}' by substituting into Equation A the known values $F_{HC} = 4500$, $F_{LC} = 500$ and $F_{HC}' = 8 F_{LC}'$:

$$(F_{LC} \times F_{HC}) = (F_{LC}' \times F_{HC}')$$
$$(500 \times 4500) = F_{LC}' \times 8F_{LC}' = 8(F_{LC}')^2$$

$$F_{LC}' = \sqrt{\frac{500 \times 4500}{8}} = 530.3 \text{ Hz}$$

Now we can find F_{HC}' by substituting into Equation A the known values:

$(F_{LC} \times F_{HC}) = (F_{LC}' \times F_{HC}')$ is $(500 \times 4500) = 530.3 \times F_{HC}'$ and

$$F_{HC}' = \frac{500 \times 4500}{530.3} = 4242.8 \text{ Hz}$$

The crossover frequencies, F_{HC}' and F_{LC}', will be used *only* to calculate the component values for the *midrange section* of the crossover. F_{HC} and F_{LC} will be used for the woofer and tweeter sections. Here are the crossover component values:

Tweeter Section (High-Pass)	Midrange Section (Bandpass)	Woofer Section (Low-Pass)
$C_1 = 159{,}155/F_{HC}R_T$ µF	$L_1 = (159.155 \times R_M)/F_{HC}'$ mH	$L_2 = (159.155 \times R_W)/F_{LC}$ mH
$C_1 = 159{,}155/4500 \times 4 = 8.8$ µF	$L_1 = 159.155 \times 8)/4242.8 = 0.3$ mH	$L_2 = (159.155 \times 8)/500 = 2.5$ mH
	$C_2 = (159{,}155/F_{LC}') \times R_M$ µF	
	$C_2 = (159{,}155/530.3) \times 8 = 37.5$ µF	

You are again advised to use impedance compensation networks, particularly for the midrange and the woofer. Although you are normally cautioned against using a -6 dB/octave crossover, it might work for the bandpass and low-pass bands. For example, the woofer and midrange may have fairly rapid natural fall-off rates which, combined with the electrical -6 dB/octave crossover rate, could give you an actual fall-off rate of -18 dB/octave. You could then apply the 18 dB/octave formulas for the 3rd-order crossover to the tweeter and end up with a complete 18 dB/octave crossover, even though the electrical filters are of mixed-order. If you are dedicated to using three drivers then, because of the complexities of a 3-way crossover bandpass section, you are advised to use PXO[2], the software program used to calculate crossover components. If you must use higher-order 3-way crossovers and lack a computer, then refer to Robert Bullock's article "Passive Crossover Networks"[3], or to Vance Dickason's *Loudspeaker Design Cookbook*. See the Appendix for access to these sources.

USING PXO TO DESIGN 3-WAY CROSSOVERS

A 3-way crossover is more difficult to design than a 2-way crossover for several reasons. First, unlike 2-way odd-order crossovers, there are no 3-way crossovers that are both All-Pass and Constant-Power. Second, there is often a *gain* in dB in the bandpass section, depending on how far apart F_{HC} and F_{LC} are placed. Precise calculation of F_{HC}' and F_{LC}' becomes more difficult as higher-order crossovers are used. Dr. Robert Bullock derived new equations for 3-way crossovers which sum to unity without having to calculate F_{HC}' or F_{LC}'. The PXO software, which is based on Bullock's equations, uses a *cascade bandpass* topology. PXO also uses another category called the *transformation bandpass* topology to eliminate low-impedance variations that can sometimes present a difficult load to the amplifier. PXO enables you to use either type of crossover topology and calculates an additional resistor to decrease any unwanted bandpass gain.

[2] *PXO Passive Crossover CAD,* Copyrighted © 1992, R. M. Bullock III
[3] R. Bullock, "Passive Crossover Networks," *Speaker Builder,* Feb. 1985

Here's an example using PXO to design a 3-way crossover for System 6 of Chapter 8. We will use the following three drivers from *Table 7-1* and *Table 4-3*: super-horn tweeter, soft-dome midrange and 8" dual-voice-coil woofer. Reviewing the frequency response and F_S of each driver, we decide to use $F_{LC} = 1500$ Hz and $F_{HC} = 6750$ Hz. The super-horn tweeter has a small voice coil and the specification sheet indicates it should be crossed over at a relatively high frequency to avoid damage. Since it would be better not to go to the very edge of the dome midrange's 10,000 Hz roll-off, using $F_{HC} = 6750$ Hz seems a good compromise. However, the bandwidth ratio is somewhat narrow, since $F_{HC}/F_{LC} = 4.5$, lower than a more preferable value of 8.

Before using PXO, recall that the crossover formulas work best when the crossover frequency is located at a place where resistance values are somewhat constant. To make this true, since the horn tweeter's and dome midrange's impedance curves definitely rise as frequencies increase, we decided to use an impedance compensation network to "flatten" the curve. In order to use impedance compensation formulas, we need information from *Table 7-1*.

Table 7-1. High-Frequency Driver Parameters

Driver Type	F_S	Q_{ES}	Q_{MS}	L_{VC}	R_E	SPL[1]
super horn tweeter	none[2]	–	–	0.269 mH	6.79 ohms	93 dB
soft dome midrange	1100 Hz	0.375	0.38	1.15 mH	7.05 ohms	89 dB
1" dome tweeter	1420 Hz	–	–	1.2 mH	6.9 ohms	92 dB

Notes: 1. SPL in units of dB/2.83V/1M   2. Horn tweeter uses Ferrofluid to damp F_S

The calculations for an impedance compensation network for the horn tweeter are as follows:

[1] $R_C = 1.25R_E = 1.25(6.79) = 8.48$ ohms (or, to the nearest tenth, 8.5 ohms)
[2] $C = 10^3(L_{VC}/R_C^2) = 10^3(0.269/8.5^2) = 3.72$ μF (or, to the nearest tenth, 3.7 μF.)

A cause for concern is using a crossover frequency close to the dome midrange's resonance, given in *Table 7-1* as $F_S = 1100$ Hz. Using $F_L = 1500$ Hz is not consistent with the advice to stay at least one octave away. This is bound to cause problems unless this resonance can be eliminated. A *series notch filter,* shown in *Figures 7-2a* and *7-2b,* can eliminate the resonant peak. The equations needed for C, L and R_N are:

$$L = 159.2 \times Q_{ES} \times R_E/F_S$$
$$C = 159{,}200/Q_{ES} \times R_E \times F_S$$
$$R_N = R_E + (Q_{ES} \times R_E/Q_{MS})$$

where:
L = inductor value in **mH**
C = capacitor value in **μF**
R_E = voice coil DC resistance in **ohms**

Substituting the values from *Table 7-1*:

$$L = 159.2(0.375)(7.05)/1100 = 0.38 \text{ mH}$$
$$C = 159{,}200/(0.375)(7.05)(1100) = 54.7 \text{ μF}$$
$$R_N = 7.05 + [(0.375)(7.05)/(0.38)] = 14 \text{ ohms}$$

The calculations for the impedance compensation network for the dome midrange are as follows:

$$R_C = 1.25(7.05) = 8.8 \text{ ohms}$$
$$C = 10^3(1.15/8.8^2) = 14.9 \text{ μF}$$

Finally, we calculate an impedance compensation network for the 8″ woofer with voice coils connected in parallel, $R_E = 2.65$ and $L_{VC} = 0.366$. Using the same equations as for the tweeter:

$$R_C = 1.25(2.65) = 3.3 \text{ ohms}$$
$$C = 10^3(0.366/3.3^2) = 33.35 \ \mu F$$

Figure 7-7 shows the PXO screen in which double arrows (>>) in the upper screen indicates that a 3-way, 2nd-order, All-Pass crossover has been selected. The rated impedances for the tweeter, midrange and woofer (R_T, R_M and R_W) are entered into the **LOADS** menu in the upper portion of *Figure 7-7*. Highlighting **BPTYPE** and pressing **Enter** opens a box that permits choice of a transformation bandpass or a cascade bandpass with or without a resistor R. The choices are: **TRNSR**, **CSCDR**, **TRNS** and **CSCD** (the last two are without a resistor). The lower center bandpass section box of *Figure 7-7* indicates that a transformation bandpass without a resistor was chosen. At the bottom of this box, a gain of 2.15 dB is indicated. This is not bad, since it will boost the midrange response, which averages 2 dB less sensitivity than the horn tweeter. If you use PXO, remember that the order of components in the bandpass section of a transformation bandpass, *Figure 7-7,* is different than that of a cascade bandpass.

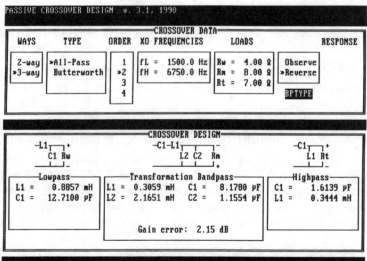

Figure 7-7. PXO Screen for All-Pass 3-Way 2nd-Order Crossover

SUMMARY

It is important to pay as much attention to crossover design as to box design. The choice of a crossover will affect the sound of a speaker system in many ways. A higher-order crossover may afford a sweeter sounding treble by a large attenuation of frequencies near a tweeter's F_S. Impedance compensation and attenuation networks will allow crossovers to act more as theory predicts. If you wish to achieve a sound close to that produced by the systems in Chapter 8, you may wish to pursue computer crossover optimization software — the current state of the art. These programs are discussed in the Appendix.

Seven Speaker System Designs

SYSTEM DESIGNS

In this concluding chapter, seven complete speaker designs are presented including a detailed description of cabinet dimensions, crossover schematics and, if a vented system is employed, port specifications. A summary of the seven systems is as follows:

2-Way Systems

1. Small closed-box satellite speaker system using a 61/2" woofer and a 1" dome tweeter.
2. Medium-sized closed-box speaker system using an 8" woofer and a 1" dome tweeter.
3. Small ported speaker system using two 4" woofers and a 1" dome tweeter positioned according to the 3/2 D'Appolito geometry.

Subwoofers

4. Large closed-box subwoofer using a 12" dual-voice-coil woofer. With the use of the appropriate crossover, this subwoofer is designed to expand the bass of either System 1 or System 2.
5. Bandpass subwoofer using two 8" dual-voice-coil subwoofers. This subwoofer is designed specifically to augment the bass of System 3.

3-Way Systems

6. Medium-sized ported 3-way speaker system using a super-horn tweeter, a 4" dome midrange, and a dual-voice-coil 8" woofer.
7. Large closed-box 3-way speaker system using two 15" woofers in an isobaric push-pull configuration and two 4" cone midranges positioned symmetrically around a 1" dome tweeter.

Required Supplies

All seven systems use drivers available at most electronics parts stores. Soldering tools, hookup wire, interconnecting wire, and speaker terminals are required to build all systems. Fiberglass packing material is required only for the closed-box systems. *Table 8-1* summarizes the common items needed.

Table 8-1. Supplies for Building Systems

Part Name	Part Name
Speaker Wire	**Speaker Terminals**
18 AWG	speaker plate (12 AWG)
16 AWG	2-position push-pull (18 AWG)
12 AWG	8-position for subwoofer
Hookup Wire	**Soldering Tools**
18 AWG	100W soldering gun
	30W soldering pencil iron
Fiberglass Packing	rosin-core solder
1 square yard	soldering paste

Speaker wire is used to connect from the speaker terminals to the amplifiers and from the crossover to the drivers. The longer the run from the amplifier to the speakers, the larger the diameter wire (i.e., smaller American Wire Gauge, or AWG) one should use. Otherwise the resistance in the wire will cause power loss before reaching the speakers. Terminals are mounted on the speakers to make convenient interconnections. Soldering tools and solder are used for internal connections for crossover components, drivers, and speaker terminals. The soldering paste keeps parts from oxidizing, thus accelerating the soldering process. The fiberglass material is stuffed into the speaker boxes to increase the apparent volume (or reduce the calculated volume) of closed box systems.

The Cabinets

If you intend to build the cabinets yourself, we recommend that you consult Chapters 4, 5, and 6 of *Speakers for Your Home and Automobile*, also published by PROMPT Publications. They provide basic information on construction and wiring techniques. One important caveat is to make sure that your final cabinets are reasonably air tight, otherwise the predictions of the speaker's bass response made by the equations or software become increasingly inaccurate. Caulk all edges on the inside of the cabinet to help ensure that the box will be air tight. In addition, use a bead of silicone rubber sealant around the holes cut for the drivers, let the bead dry, mount the drivers, and screw them in place to provide an air tight seal.

If you cannot build the enclosures yourself, there are several places that specialize in building cabinets to specifications. Some are given in the Appendix. Speaker cabinets can be custom built in 3/4" or 1" MDF (medium density fiberboard) and finished in either Formica® or real wood veneer, such as oak or walnut. You can specify either sharp or rounded edges on either rectangular or slanted cabinets. Cabinet dimensions, driver diameters and terminals must be specified, along with port diameter and length if a vented box is to be built. One manufacturer specializes in building rectangular speaker cabinets with rounded edges and gives them a high-tech modern look by finishing them in a granular nextel paint. Some manufacturers supply custom-built grilles on all orders and may even have available capacitors, inductors, resistors, drivers, terminals, ports and kits. If you write or call, they usually will send you more information.

Crossover Electronics

In general, after calculating the component values for the crossover desired for a design, you will not be able to purchase resistors and capacitors in the precise values specified. You will need to combine resistors and capacitors which have values that you can purchase to form the required values. Review Chapter 1 for a refresher on how to combine capacitors and resistors in series and/or parallel to develop the values needed for a specific crossover. Inductors, on the other hand, are always purchased at or close to the exact value needed. To build the custom crossovers required by the seven systems in the chapter, you will need access to sources which can provide an extensive variety of capacitors, inductors and resistors.

Table 8-2 lists component parts to build custom crossovers. The inductor is a fairly large value, the capacitors are nonpolarized electrolytic capacitors, and the resistors have a wattage rating suitable for crossovers.

Table 8-2. Component Parts for Crossovers

L	C	R
4.2 mH	1 µF	1 Ω, 10W
	2.2 µF	8 Ω, 20W
	4.7 µF	10 Ω, 10W
	10 µF	

If your local parts store does not have the resistor or capacitor value that you need in stock, you might have to special order it.

Exact value inductors are a special problem. Small inductors are wound on plastic air-core bobbins. Large inductors are wound on ferrite cores to ensure large values of inductance while maintaining low resistance in series with the driver. Several excellent sources that specialize in audio system components, especially those for crossover designs, are listed in the Appendix. They can supply a wide range of standard inductors, custom-wound inductors, a wide variety of polypropylene, mylar, and electrolytic capacitors, and many different resistor values. For example, the large 34 mH or 44mH inductors used in System 4 can be custom ordered from the Meniscus Audio Group using a "strangler" ferrite core with either 18 AWG or 16 AWG wire. In addition, Madisound Speaker Components offers eleven iron core inductors which use 20 AWG or 18 AWG wire, and over 100 inductors which use 14 AWG or 15 AWG wires.

Crossover Construction

All of the crossover parts can be glued onto the smooth side of a masonite board using an adhesive, such as one used to glue paneling to walls. After all the glued components on the board are wired together and speaker wires for the drivers and terminals are connected, all of the connections can be soldered. The appropriate wires from the crossover(s) must be long enough to reach the drivers and terminals. The completed board can then be permanently fastened to the cabinet using screws or hot glue. The final steps include screwing the drivers and terminals in place and soldering wires to the drivers and terminals. In some cases, capacitors already fastened to the tweeter must be removed before attaching the wires from the crossover.

DESIGN OF SYSTEM 1

Here is an overall summary of System 1. The cabinet layout is shown in *Figure 8-1a,* a schematic of the crossover network is shown in *Figure 8-1b,* and the final bass response of the woofer is shown in *Figure 8-1c.* System 1 can be used with System 4.

SYSTEM 1 — Small Sealed 2-Way Satellite System

SYSTEM SPECIFICATIONS:

Enclosure type:	Sealed box (0.264 ft³)	Crossover Frequency:	2200 Hz
−3 dB frequency:	74 Hz	Crossover Rate:	18 dB/octave
Peak response:	4.33 dB @ 125 Hz	Speaker sensitivity:	88 dB/2.83V/1m

DRIVERS:
The tweeters and woofers used in this system are as follows:

Type	Size	Quantity
Dome tweeter (8Ω)	1"	2
Polypropylene woofer (8Ω)	6½"	2

CABINETS:
Figure 8-1a illustrates the cabinet layout and gives the center location and radius of each driver opening. The cabinet dimensions are as follows:

Quantity	Wall Thickness	Inside Dimensions H × W × D	Outside Dimensions H × W × D
2	3/4"	12" × 6¾" × 5⅝"	13½" × 8¼" × 7⅛""

ACCESSORIES:
In addition to the soldering tools, solder, and hookup wire listed in *Table 8-1,* the following accessories are required for this system:

Item	Quantity	Comments
Fiber Glass Stuffing	2	Use one bag per speaker
Terminals	2	Fits 12-gauge speaker wire

CROSSOVER ELECTRONICS:
Figure 8-1b shows a schematic diagram for the crossover. Each part and the quantity needed for a pair of speakers is as follows:

Capacitors	Quantity	Inductors	Quantity	Resistors	Quantity
8 µF	2	0.4 mH	2	3 Ω	2
10 µF	2	0.57 mH	2	8 Ω	2
13 µF	2	0.7 mH	2		

A 61/2" woofer is a natural candidate for a small 2-way system. *Figure 8-2* shows its frequency response. Since the woofer's response is erratic above 3000 Hz, a crossover point was chosen between 2000 and 3000 Hz. A 1" dome tweeter can respond down to this region, making it a satisfactory companion. Since the tweeter has its fundamental resonance at 1420 Hz, a 3rd-order crossover calculated at a crossover frequency of 2200 Hz should prevent excitation of this resonance. Recall that 3rd-order crossovers provide sharp filtering at the rate of 18 dB/octave.

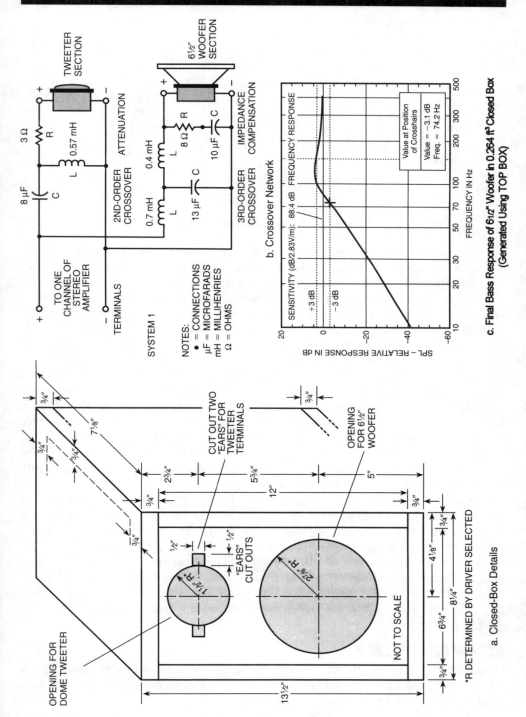

Figure 8-1. System 1 — Small Closed-Box 2-Way Satellite Speaker System

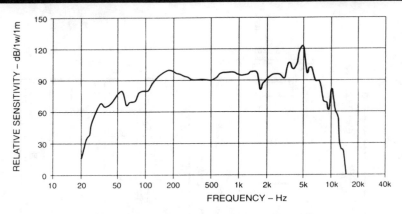

Figure 8-2. Frequency Response of 6½" Woofer

Advanced crossover optimization software was used to select components for the System 1 crossover network shown in *Figure 8-1b*. Note that the tweeter circuity is a 2nd-order crossover circuit and the woofer circuity is a 3rd-order crossover circuit. The frequency response and impedance curve information for the 6½" woofer was entered into the optimization program with the aim of achieving the target acoustic rolloff of 18 dB/octave. The results of tailoring the network are shown in *Figures 8-3a, 8-3b,* and *8-3c.* In these three figures, the original system response curve is represented by a dotted line, the ideal target crossover response is represented by a dashed line, and the predicted crossover response is represented as a solid line. *Figure 8-3a* shows a sharp peak in the predicted crossover response at 2000 Hz when using a crossover calculated solely by using the equations described in Chapter 7. This peak is cut down, as shown in *Figure 8-3b,* when an impedance compensation network, calculated using equations of Chapter 7, is included in the crossover circuit. Adding adjusted computer optimized crossover components to the impedance compensation network, the predicted response now agrees closely with the target curve as shown in *Figure 8-3c.*

Figure 8-4 shows the frequency response of the 1" dome tweeter as measured by an FFT (Fast Fourier Transform) system known as MLSSA[1]. After 2000 Hz, the tweeter's sensitivity averages slightly above 90 dB, forcing use of a series 3-ohm resistor in the tweeter crossover circuit to attenuate the tweeter's response by 2 dB in order to match the woofer's 88 dB sensitivity. The crossover is optimized to work with the increased resistance resulting from the use of this 3-ohm resistor. The final bass response of the 6½" woofer using the sealed box specified is shown in *Figure 8-1c.* The box volume was calculated based on using a square yard of fiberglass stuffing per box.

DESIGN OF SYSTEM 2

Here is an overall summary of System 2. The cabinet layout is shown in *Figure 8-5a,* a schematic of the crossover network is shown in *Figure 8-5b,* and the final bass response of the woofer is shown in *Figure 8-5c.*

[1] MLSSA, DRA Laboratories

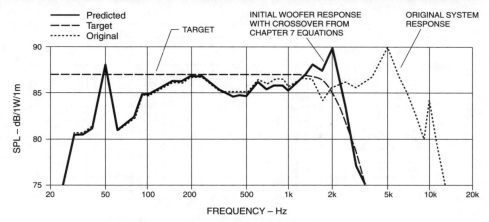

a. Original System 1 – Initial and Targeted Woofer Responses

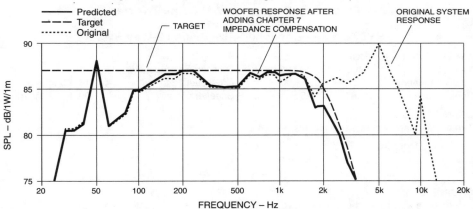

b. Woofer Response After Adding Impedance Compensation Components

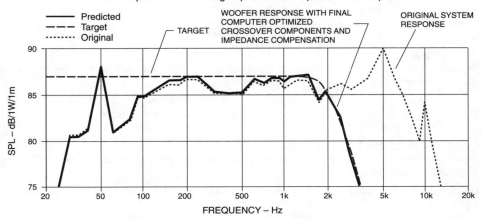

c. Final Woofer Response Using Computer Optimized Components

Figure 8-3. System 1 Woofer Responses

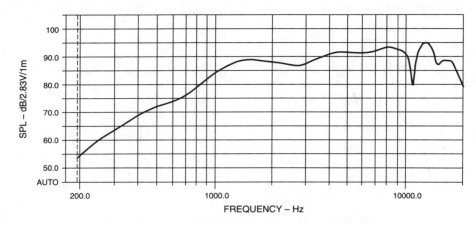

Figure 8-4. Frequency Response of 1" Dome Tweeter

SYSTEM 2 — Bookshelf-Size Sealed 2-Way System

SYSTEM SPECIFICATIONS:

Enclosure type:	Sealed box (0.635 ft³)	Crossover Frequency:	2200 Hz
−3 dB frequency:	57.6 Hz	Crossover Rate:	18 dB/octave
Peak response:	2.88 dB @ 95 Hz	Speaker sensitivity:	90 dB/2.83V/1m

DRIVERS:
The tweeters and woofers used in this system are as follows:

Quantity	Type	Size
2	Dome tweeter (8Ω)	1"
2	Polypropylene woofer (8Ω)	8"

CABINETS:
Figure 8-5a illustrates the cabinet layout and gives the center location and radius of each driver opening. The cabinet dimensions are as follows:

Quantity	Wall Thickness	Inside Dimensions H × W × D	Outside Dimensions H × W × D
2	3/4"	16¼" × 10" × 6¾""	17¾" × 11½" × 8¼""

ACCESSORIES:
In addition to the soldering tools, solder, and hookup wire listed in *Table 8-1,* the following accessories are required for this system:

Item	Quantity	Comments
Fiber Glass Stuffing	2	Use one bag per speaker
Terminals	2	Fits 12-gauge

CROSSOVER ELECTRONICS:
Figure 8-5b shows a schematic diagram for the crossover. Each part and the quantity needed for a pair of speakers is as follows:

Capacitors	Quantity	Inductors	Quantity	Resistors	Quantity
8 µF	2	0.57 mH	2	2 Ω	2
36 µF	2	0.65 mH	2	7 Ω	2

The tweeter used is the same as for System 1. We continue to use this 1" dome tweeter at a crossover frequency of 2200 Hz because the woofers used showed er-

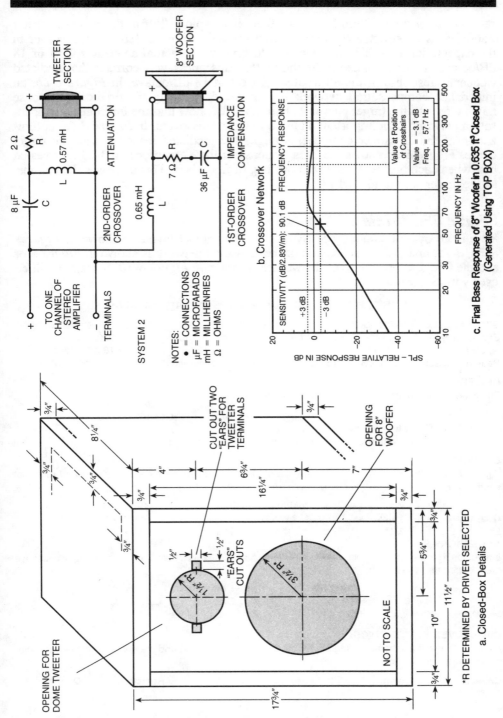

Figure 8-5. System 2 Bookshelf-Size Closed-Box 2-Way Speaker System

ratic behavior above 2500 Hz. Since there is a rapid rolloff in the 8" woofer after 2500 Hz, we instructed the optimization software to use a 1st-order crossover in the expectation that this crossover would generate an actual acoustic rolloff of 18 dB/octave. Indeed, *Figure 8-6a* shows that this guess was correct; the predicted frequency response of the 8" woofer calls off at 18 dB/octave. In *Figure 8-6b*, an impedance compensation network is introduced, bringing the predicted response much closer to the target curve. It should be clear now that the impedance compensation network is an important addition to most crossovers. In *Figure 8-6c*, optimization of the crossover components aligns the predicted response with the target curve. *Figure 8-5c* shows the bass response of the 8" woofer in a 17.8 liter sealed box when each box is stuffed with one bag of fiberglass. This increases the volume, as the driver sees it, to 18.1 liters.

DESIGN OF SYSTEM 3

Here is an overall summary of System 3. The cabinet layout is shown in *Figures 8-7a, 8-7b,* and *8-7c*, a schematic of the crossover network is shown in *Figure 8-8*, and the final bass response of the woofer is shown in *Figure 8-10*. System 3 will be used with System 5.

SYSTEM 3 — Small Ported 3/2 Geometry Satellites

SYSTEM SPECIFICATIONS:

Enclosure type:	Ported box (0.257 ft³)	Crossover Frequency:	2200 Hz
–3 dB frequency:	118 Hz	Crossover Rate:	18 dB/octave
Peak response:	6.8 dB @ 175 Hz	Speaker sensitivity:	91.5 dB/2.83V/1m

DRIVERS:
The tweeters and woofers used in this system are as follows:

Type	Size	Quantity
Dome tweeter (8Ω)	1"	2
Paper-cone midrange woofer (8Ω)	4"	4

CABINETS:
Figure 8-7a, 8-7b, and *8-7c* illustrates the cabinet layout and gives the center location and radius of each driver opening. The cabinet dimensions are as follows:

Quantity	Wall Thickness	Inside Dimensions H × W × D	Outside Dimensions H × W × D
2	3/4"	13½" × 4½" × 7⁵⁄₁₆"	15" × 6" × 8¹³⁄₁₆"

ACCESSORIES:
In addition to the soldering tools, solder, and hookup wire listed in *Table 8-1,* the following accessories are required for this system:

Item	Quantity	Comments
Ports	4	Diameter = 2", L_v = 31/32"
Terminals	2	Fits 12-gauge

CROSSOVER ELECTRONICS:
Figure 8-8 shows a schematic diagram for the crossover. Each part and the quantity needed for a pair of speakers is as follows:

Capacitors	Quantity	Inductors	Quantity	Resistors	Quantity
8 μF	2	0.57 mH	2	2 Ω	2
25 μF	2	0.2 mH	2	4.3 Ω	2
17 μF	2	0.18 mH	2		

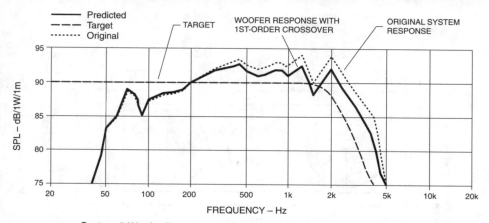

a. System 2 Woofer Responses – Original, Target and 1st-Order Crossover

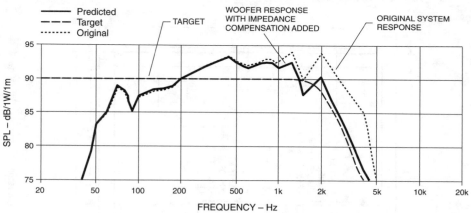

b. Woofer Response with Impedance Compensation Added to Crossover

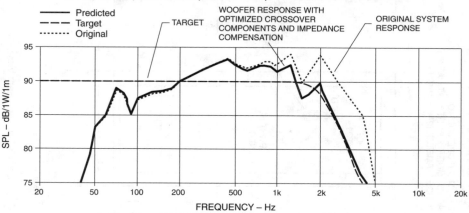

c. Final Woofer Response Using Computer Optimized Components

Figure 8-6. System 2 Woofer Responses

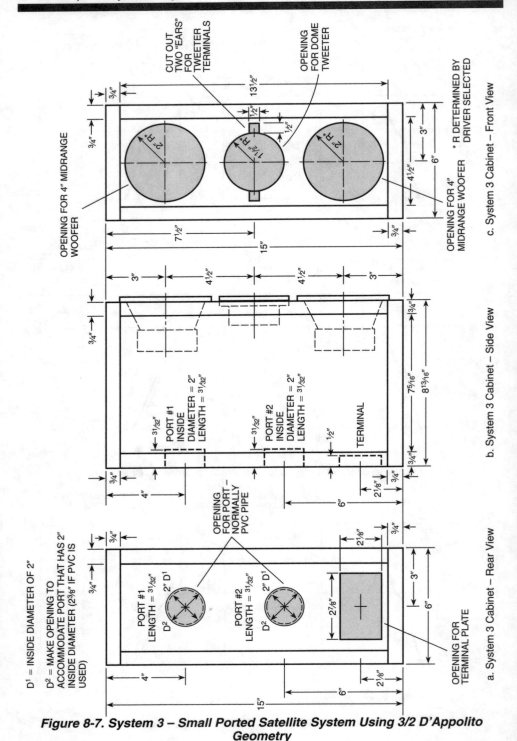

Figure 8-7. System 3 – Small Ported Satellite System Using 3/2 D'Appolito Geometry

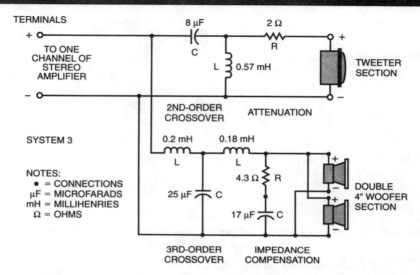

Figure 8-8. System 3 — Small Ported Satellite System Using 3/2 D'Appolito Geometry

System 3 continues to use the same basic tweeter as System 1 and System 2. The frequency response and impedance curve for two 4" paper-cone midrange woofers driven in parallel were entered into the crossover optimization program. We wish the woofer response to achieve an acoustic rolloff of 18 dB/octave at 2200 Hz. *Figure 8-9* shows that attempting to use a 2nd-order crossover, even with impedance compensation, falls short of aligning with the target response curve. However, when we use a 3rd-order crossover with impedance compensation and optimization, as shown in *Figure 8-10,* a close alignment with the target response curve is obtained. *Figure 6-9* at the end of Chapter 6 shows the bass response of this satellite system.

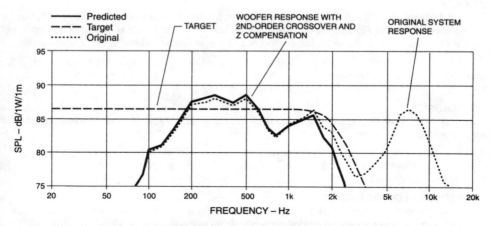

Figure 8-9. System 3 Woofer Response — Original, Target and 2nd-Order Crossover With Impedance Compensation

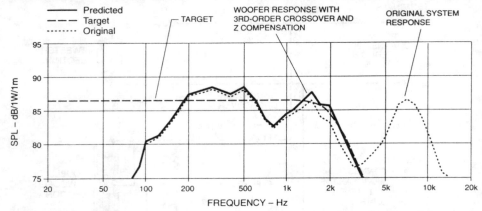

Figure 8-10. System 3 Woofer Response with Optimized 3rd-Order Crossover and Impedance Compensation

SYSTEM 4 DESIGN AND CONSTRUCTION

Here is an overall summary of System 4. The cabinet design and construction is shown in *Figures 8-11a,* an assembled box is shown in *Figure 8-11b,* and the subwoofer internal wiring is shown in *Figure 8-12.*

SYSTEM 4 — Dual-Voice-Coil Subwoofer (Designed to work with System 1)

SYSTEM SPECIFICATIONS: As designed to work with System 1

Enclosure type:	Sealed box (6.8 ft³)	Crossover Frequency:	74 Hz
−3 dB frequency:	29 Hz	Crossover Rate:	12 dB/octave
Peak response:	1.75 dB @ 50 Hz	Speaker sensitivity:	96 dB/2.83V/1m

DRIVER:
The subwoofer used in this system is as follows:

Type	Size	Quantity
Dual-voice-coil subwoofer (8Ω)	12″	1

CABINET:
Figure 8-11 details the cabinet dimensions and construction and gives the center location and radius for the driver opening. See *Figure 8-11* and the following text for assembly steps and a full description of cabinet construction. The sealed enclosure dimensions are as follows, additional sides are attached:

Quantity	Wall Thickness	Inside Dimensions H×W×D	Outside Dimensions H×W×D
1	3/4″	32″ × 21½″ × 14½″	33½″ × 23″ × 16″

ACCESSORIES:
In addition to the soldering tools, solder, and hookup wire listed in *Table 8-1,* the following accessories are required for this system:

Item	Quantity	Comments
Fiber Glass Stuffing	5	Fill entire enclosure
Terminals	1	8-position terminal

CROSSOVER ELECTRONICS:
Figure 8-12a shows a schematic diagram for the crossover and internal connections for the subwoofer. Each part and the quantity needed for one subwoofer is as follows:

Capacitors	Quantity	Inductors	Quantity	Resistors	Quantity
134 µF	2	34 mH	2	None	

Inside Dimensions of Closed Box: 32″ H x 21½″ W x 14½″ D
Closed Box Outside Dimensions: 33½″ H x 23″ W x 16″ D

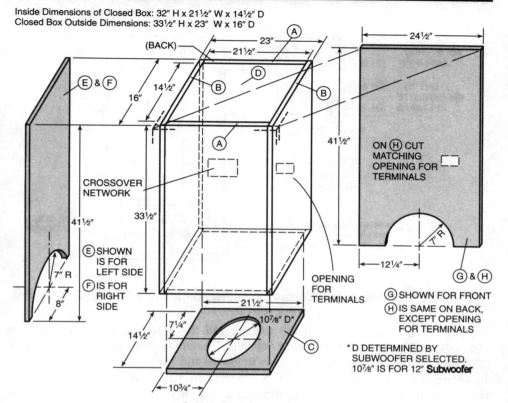

a. Cabinet Design and Construction

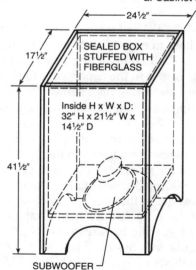

b. Upside Down Driver Mounting

SYSTEM 4 ASSEMBLY STEPS
(All material is 3/4″ thick.)
Closed-Box Construction

1. Cut two panels (A) 21½″ W x 33½″ H for front and back
2. Cut two panels (B) 16″ W x 33½″ H for sides.
3. Cut two panels 21½″ W x 14½″ D. (D) is for top; (C) is for bottom. In (C), cut opening for subwoofer 40-1350 from Radio Shack.
4. Mount subwoofer to bottom (C). Seal it properly.
5. Temporarily assemble front and back (A) and sides (B) to bottom (C).
6. Decide where the crossover network is to be mounted and where the terminals will bring wires from closed box. Cut the openings in the appropriate panels [most likely (H) and the back panel (A)].
7. Glue and screw front, back, and sides to bottom. Seal all inside joints with caulk.
8. Mount crossover network and terminals. Connect all wires, double-check connections, then solder all connections.
9. Stuff enclosure with fiberglass.
10. Glue and screw top in place.

Outside Panels

11. Glue and screw sides (E) and (F) and front (G) and back (H) in place.

Figure 8-11. System 4 Dual-Voice-Coil Subwoofer

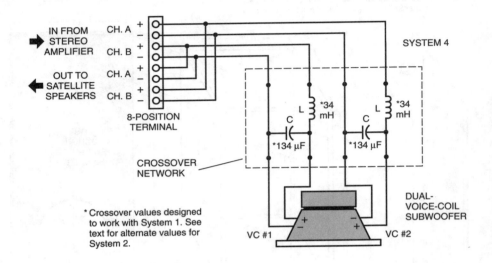

Figure 8-12. System 4 Dual-Voice-Coil Subwoofer Internal Wiring (Designed to Work with System 1)

The detailed dimensions of the cabinet and the assembly steps are given in *Figure 8-11*. First construct the basic cabinet with outside dimensions 33½" × 23" × 16". Leave off the top until the bottom is mounted and the cabinet is sealed. The 12" dual-voice-coil driver is mounted in the bottom in an opening of diameter 10⅞". Mount the crossover network and terminals and interconnect the components as shown in *Figure 8-12*. Carefully stuff the closed box with the fiberglass filler. Then secure the top.

Cut out four panels, two of dimensions 41½" × 24½" and the other two of dimensions 41½" × 16". Locate the center point of the bottom edge of each panel. From this center point, draw a semi-circle of radius 7" at the bottom of all four panels. Cut out the semi-circle with a saber saw. Attach the four panels to the appropriate four sides of the cabinet with screws and glue. You will now have a 41½" high subwoofer cabinet on legs with sides 1½" thick, which helps to suppress panel resonances. The completed assembly should look like *Figure 8-11b*.

The crossover is a 12 dB/octave low-pass design, calculated using $R_W = 8$ ohms and a crossover frequency of 74 Hz. This offers a smooth transition to the $F_3 = 74$ Hz of System 1, which has a response that drops off at the rate of 12 dB/octave below the sealed box F_3. The sensitivity of the subwoofer is rated much higher than that of System 1. However, if the subwoofer is placed well into the room, diffraction losses will bring this sensitivity down close to that of the satellites. Refer to Chapter 6 to recall how the bass response was designed. The specific bass response is given in *Figure 6-6*. If you wish to have this subwoofer work with System 2 instead of System 1, then the crossover must be changed to match the F_3 of System 2, which is 57.6 Hz. In this case you would need to use two inductors, each with a value of 44 mH, and two capacitors, each with a value of 173 µF. The two systems are interconnected as shown in *Figure 6-4*.

SYSTEM 5 DESIGN AND CONSTRUCTION

Here is an overall summary of System 5. The cabinet details and assembly steps are given in *Figure 8-13*, and the wiring of the dual-voice-coil subwoofers in push-pull is shown in *Figure 8-14*.

Assemble the cabinet detailed in *Figure 8-13* according to the steps given. This bandpass subwoofer requires no crossover network so the wiring is just between the dual-voice-coil subwoofers and the terminals as shown in *Figure 8-14*. The Channel A and Channel B voice coils on each subwoofer are driven out of phase for the push-pull action required. A photograph of System 5 with System 3 satellite speakers on top is shown in *Figure 8-15*.

The main concern with a bandpass subwoofer is to make sure that the drivers on the partition, and the partition itself between the sealed cabinet and the vented portion, are well caulked so that no air leaks take place. The bandpass subwoofer does not require a crossover to pass a band of frequencies. The box itself acts as an acoustic crossover. For further discussion and explanation of how this bandpass subwoofer was designed, refer to Chapter 6. The bandpass response between frequencies of 45 Hz and 115 Hz is shown in *Figure 6-9*.

SYSTEM 5 — Bandpass Subwoofer (Designed to work with System 3)[2]

SYSTEM SPECIFICATIONS: As designed to work with System 3

Enclosure type:	Ported Bandpass Subwoofer	Crossover:	None
Lower –3 dB frequency:	45 Hz	Response Peak:	0.277 dB
Upper –3 dB frequency:	115 Hz	Speaker sensitivity:	98.7 dB/2.83V/1m

DRIVERS:

The two subwoofers used in this system are mounted in opposite directions on the inner partition to implement the isobaric push-pull design.

Type	Size	Quantity
Dual-voice-coil subwoofer (8Ω)	8″	2

CABINET:

Figure 8-13 illustrates the cabinet details and gives the center locations and radii of the subwoofer and port openings. The inside partition is located 12⁵⁄₁₆″ from one side of the enclosure. No drivers are exposed to the outside; only the ports, as shown in *Figure 8-13*. The cabinet dimensions are as follows:

Quantity	Wall Thickness	Inside Dimensions H×W×D	Outside Dimensions H×W×D
1	3/4″	22″ × 23¾″ × 12″	23½″ × 25¼″ × 13½″

ACCESSORIES:

In addition to the soldering tools, solder, and hookup wire listed in *Table 8-1*, the following accessories are required for this system:

Item	Quantity	Comments
Ports	2	Diameter = 4″, L_v = 2³⁵⁄₆₄″
Terminals	1	8-position terminal

CROSSOVER ELECTRONICS:

No crossover is required. See *Figure 8-14* for the internal wiring of the bandpass subwoofer.

Capacitors	Quantity	Inductors	Quantity	Resistors	Quantity
None		None		None	

---

[2] System 5 paired with System 3 forms a low impedance system. A high-current amplifier is recommended, particularly when listening to pop music at high SPLs.

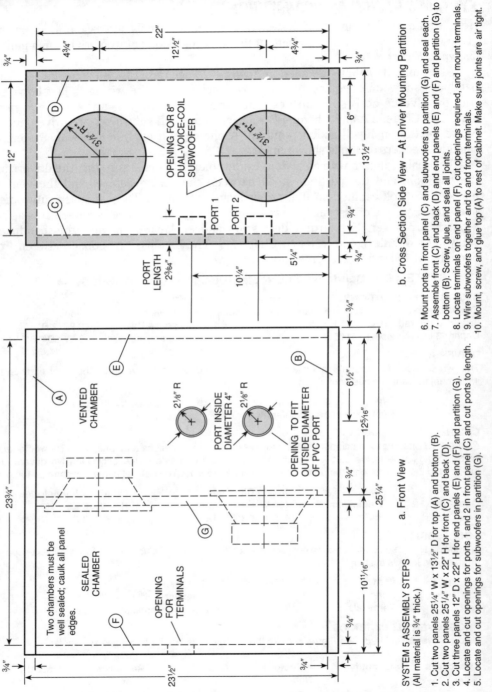

Figure 8-13. System 5 Bandpass Subwoofer (45 Hz to 115 Hz) (Designed to work with System 3)

b. Cross Section Side View – At Driver Mounting Partition

6. Mount ports in front panel (C) and subwoofers to partition (G) and seal each.
7. Assemble front (C) and back (D) and end panels (E) and (F) and partition (G) to bottom (B). Screw, glue, and seal all joints.
8. Locate terminals on end panel (F), cut openings required, and mount terminals.
9. Wire subwoofers together and to and from terminals.
10. Mount, screw, and glue top (A) to rest of cabinet. Make sure joints are air tight.

a. Front View

SYSTEM 5 ASSEMBLY STEPS
(All material is 3/4" thick.)

1. Cut two panels 25 1/4" W x 13 1/2" D for top (A) and bottom (B).
2. Cut two panels 25 1/4" W x 22" H for front (C) and back (D).
3. Cut three panels 12" D x 22" H for end panels (E) and (F) and partition (G).
4. Locate and cut openings for ports 1 and 2 in front panel (C) and cut ports to length.
5. Locate and cut openings for subwoofers in partition (G).

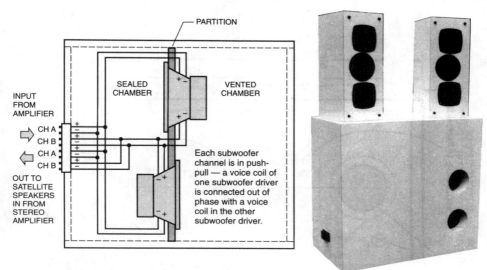

Figure 8-14. System 5 Bandpass Subwoofer (45 Hz to 115 Hz) (Designed to work with System 3)

Figure 8-15. System 5 with System 3 on Top

SYSTEM 6 DESIGN AND CONSTRUCTION

Here is an overall summary of System 6. The cabinet details are shown in *Figure 8-16* and the crossover network is shown in *Figure 8-17*. The assembly steps are given in *Figure 8-18a* and the bass response is shown in *Figure 8-18b*.

SYSTEM 6 — Medium-Size Ported 3-Way System

SYSTEM SPECIFICATIONS:

Enclosure type:	Ported box (1.049 ft³)	Crossover Frequencies:	1500 Hz, 6750 Hz
–3 dB frequency:	52 Hz	Crossover Rate:	12 dB/octave
Peak response:	5 dB @ 90 Hz	Speaker sensitivity:	91 dB/2.83V/1m

DRIVERS:
The drivers used in this system are as follows:

Type	Size	Quantity
Super Horn tweeter (8 Ω)		2
Dome midrange (8 Ω)	4″	2
Dual-voice-coil subwoofer (8 Ω)	8″	2

CABINET:
Figure 8-16 details the cabinet dimensions and gives the center location and radius of each driver opening on the front panel. Ports and terminals are located on the back of the cabinet. The cabinet dimensions are as follows:

Quantity	Wall Thickness	Inside Dimensions H×W×D	Outside Dimensions H×W×D
2	3/4″	22″ × 11½″ × 8½″	23½″ × 13″ × 10″

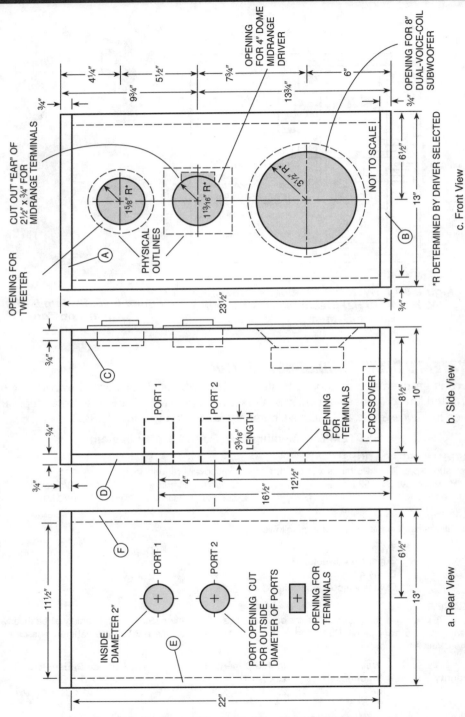

Figure 8-16. System 6 Medium-Size Ported 3-Way System

ACCESSORIES:
In addition to the soldering tools, solder, and hookup wire listed in *Table 8-1,* the following accessories are required for this system:

Item	Quantity	Comments
Ports	4	Diameter = 2″, L_v = 3³⁄₁₆″
Terminals	2	

CROSSOVER ELECTRONICS:
Figure 8-17 shows a schematic diagram for the crossover. Each part and the quantity needed for a pair of speakers is as follows:

Capacitors	Quantity	Inductors	Quantity	Resistors	Quantity
1.6 µF	2	0.35 mH	2	8 Ω	2
4 µF	2	0.3 mH	2	8.8 Ω	2
8 µF	2	2 mH	2	3.3 Ω	2
1 µF	2	0.4 mH	2	14 Ω	2
55 µF	2	0.9 mH	2		
15 µF	2				
13 µF	2				
33 µF	2				

The crossover for System 6 was developed by using both equations and sophisticated crossover software[2]. The software calculates a bandpass gain for the midrange, resulting from both the crossover and the spread of the crossover frequencies. This bandpass gain more closely matches the midrange sensitivity to that of the tweeter. Since this is a 12 dB/octave three-way crossover, remember to *reverse the polarity of the midrange only.*

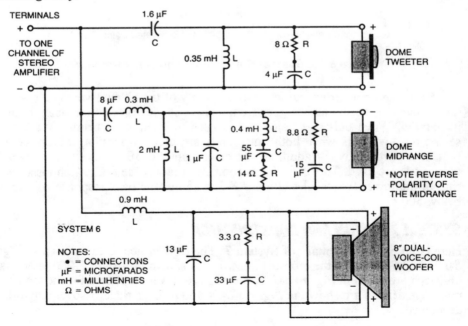

Figure 8-17. System 6 Medium-Size Ported 3-Way System

[2] PXO, Old Colony Sound Lab

SYSTEM 6 ASSEMBLY STEPS
(All material is 3/4" thick.)

1. Cut two panels 13" W x 10" D for top (A) and bottom (B).
2. Cut two panels 13" W x 22" H for front (C) and back (D).
3. Cut two panels 8½" D x 22" H for side panels (E) and (F).
4. Locate and cut openings for tweeter, midrange, and woofer in front panel (C).
5. Locate and cut openings for ports 1 and 2 in back panel (D) and cut ports to length; also locate terminals and cut openings in back as required.
6. Assemble ports in back panel (D) and three drivers to front panel (C) and seal each.
7. Assemble front (C), back (D), and side panels (E) and (F) to bottom (B). Screw, glue, and seal all joints.
8. Assemble crossover network, wire together components, and locate it in cabinet.
9. Mount terminals on back panel (D). Solder wires from crossover network to tweeter, midrange, and woofer drivers and to terminals.
10. Mount, glue, and screw top (A) to rest of cabinet.
11. Make sure joints are airtight.

a. Assembly Steps

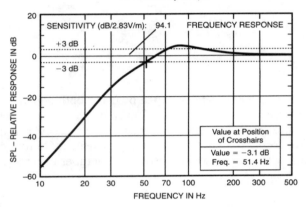

b. System 6 Bass Response Below 500 Hz (Generated Using TOP BOX)

Figure 8-18. System 6 Assembly and Bass Response

As pointed out earlier, an interesting quality of the 8" dual-voice-coil woofer is the change that occurs as one goes from using a single voice coil to using both coils in parallel. When only one voice coil is used, this driver is primarily suited to a sealed box, whereas when both voice coils are used in parallel, the driver works best in a ported box. In addition, the driver gains 6 dB in sensitivity when both voice coils are used. This is useful in compensating for the diffraction losses occurring in the lower frequencies. *Figure 8-18b* shows the bass response of System 6 below 500 Hz.

SYSTEM 7 DESIGN AND CONSTRUCTION

Here is an overall summary of System 7. The cabinet details are shown in *Figures 8-19a* and *8-20a*, and the crossover network is shown in *Figure 8-20b*. The assembly steps are given in *Figure 8-19b*, and the crossover responses for the woofer and midrange drivers are shown in *Figures 8-21* and *8-22* as the crossover network was developed.

SYSTEM 7 — Large Floor-Standing Sealed Isobaric P-P 3-Way System

SYSTEM SPECIFICATIONS:

Enclosure type:	Sealed box (3.55 ft³) with panels	Crossover Frequencies:	275 Hz, 2200 Hz
−3 dB frequency:	27 Hz	Crossover Rate:	12 dB/octave, 18 db/octave
Peak response:	1.6 dB @ 55 Hz	Speaker sensitivity:	92 dB/2.83V/1m

DRIVERS:

The woofers are connected in isobaric push-pull. The drivers used in this system are as follows:

Type	Size	Quantity
Dome tweeter (8 Ω)	1″	2
Paper-cone midrange (8 Ω)	4″	4
Poly-cone woofer (8 Ω)	15″	4

CABINETS:

Figures 8-19a and *8-20a* show the cabinet details and give the center location and radius of each driver opening. The assembly steps for construction are listed in *Figure 8-19b*. The total cabinet is a front, back, two end panels, and a top surrounding a sealed box. The cabinet dimensions given below are only for the sealed box portion of the cabinet. The sealed box is stuffed with fiberglass to increase effective box volume. The 19½″ × 41″ front and back panels and two 18″ × 41″ panels, plus a 19½″ × 19½″ top provide an overall cabinet with outside dimensions of 19½″ (W) × 41¾″ (H) × 19½″ (D). The cabinet with drivers mounted, but without grille screens, is shown in *Figure 8-20c*.

Quantity	Wall Thickness	Sealed Box Inside Dimensions H × W × D	Sealed Box Outside Dimensions H × W × D
2	3/4″	22½″ × 16½″ × 16½″	24″ × 18″ × 18″

ACCESSORIES:

In addition to the soldering tools, solder, and hookup wire listed in *Table 8-1*, the following accessories are required for this system:

Item	Quantity	Comments
Fiberglass	10	5 bags in each box
Terminals	2	
15″ grille screens	6	For cabinet cutouts
Grille cloth	1	36″ × 34″ sheet
Grille frame	1	19½″ × 20″ from 1″ × 3/4″ stock
Heavy duty casters	8	Four per cabinet
Large plastic cups	4	One behind each midrange

CROSSOVER ELECTRONICS:

Figure 8-20b shows a schematic diagram for the crossover. Each part and the quantity needed for a pair of speakers is as follows:

Capacitors	Quantity	Inductors	Quantity	Resistors	Quantity
8 µF	2	0.57 mH	2	2 Ω	2
76 µF	2	0.3 mH	2	4.3 Ω	2
18 µF	2	0.2 mH	2	3.5 Ω	2
17 µF	2	2.8 mH	2		
120 µF	2				
150 µF	2				

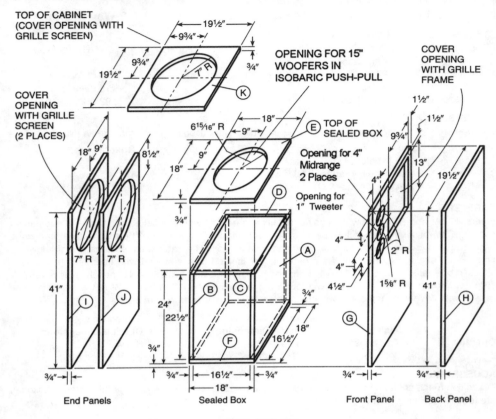

a. Cabinet Details

SYSTEM 7 ASSEMBLY STEPS
(All material is ¾" thick.)

Sealed Box
1. Cut two panels 18″ × 22½″ for front (A) and back (B).
2. Cut two panels 16 1/2″ × 22½″ for end panels (C) and (D).
3. Cut two panels 18″ × 18″ for top (E) and bottom (F).
4. Assemble front (A), back (B), and end panels (C) and (D) to bottom (F). Glue and screw in place. Seal all inside joints with caulk.
5. Locate and cut opening in top (E) for woofers. Radius is 6¹⁵⁄₁₆″ for 15″ woofer RS 40-1301.
6. Mount the subwoofers back-to-back on top (E) as shown in *Figure 8-20a.* Seal each properly.
7. Drill holes in top (E), pass wires through, and solder voice coils of woofers in push-pull as shown in crossover network schematic.
8. Stuff box with fiberglass filler, then glue and screw top (E) in place.

Total Cabinet
1. Cut two panels 19½″ × 41″ for front (G) and back (H).
2. Cut two panels 18″ × 41″ for end panels (I) and (J).
3. Cut panel 19½″ × 19½″ for top (K).
4. Locate and cut openings in top (K), and end panels (I) and (J).
5. Locate and cut openings in front (G) for tweeter, midrange drivers and rectangular opening.
6. Mount tweeter and midrange drivers in front (G).
7. Assemble front (G), back (H), and two end panels (I) and (J) to sealed box. Screw panels in place.
8. Assemble the crossover network and decide on its position and mount it in cabinet.
9. Decide on position of terminals, cut opening in back panel (H) for terminals, and mount terminals.
10. Wire tweeter, midranges, woofers and terminals to crossover network.
11. Build the grille frame and cover with grille cloth. Mount all grille screens and grille frame to front (G), end panels (I) and (J) and top (K).
12. Mount the heavy-duty casters to the bottom (F) of cabinet.

b. Assembly Steps

Figure 8-19. System 7 Cabinet Details and Assembly Steps

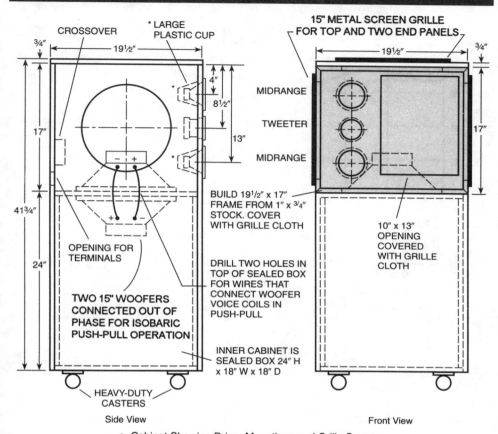

CROSSOVER | *** LARGE PLASTIC CUP**

15" METAL SCREEN GRILLE FOR TOP AND TWO END PANELS

3/4"

19½"

4"

8½"

13"

MIDRANGE

TWEETER

MIDRANGE

17"

41¾"

24"

OPENING FOR TERMINALS

BUILD 19½" x 17" FRAME FROM 1" x ¾" STOCK. COVER WITH GRILLE CLOTH

10" x 13" OPENING COVERED WITH GRILLE CLOTH

DRILL TWO HOLES IN TOP OF SEALED BOX FOR WIRES THAT CONNECT WOOFER VOICE COILS IN PUSH-PULL

TWO 15" WOOFERS CONNECTED OUT OF PHASE FOR ISOBARIC PUSH-PULL OPERATION

INNER CABINET IS SEALED BOX 24" H x 18" W x 18" D

HEAVY-DUTY CASTERS

Side View | Front View

a. Cabinet Showing Driver Mountings and Grille Screens

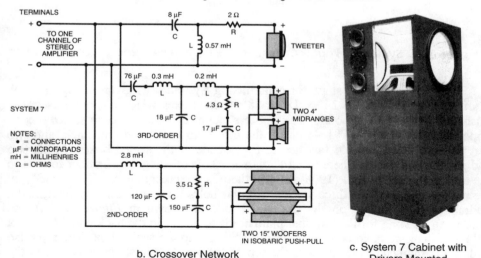

TERMINALS

TO ONE CHANNEL OF STEREO AMPLIFIER

8 µF C | 2 Ω R | L 0.57 mH | TWEETER

76 µF C | 0.3 mH L | 0.2 mH L | 4.3 Ω R | TWO 4" MIDRANGES

18 µF C | 17 µF C

3RD-ORDER

2.8 mH L

3.5 Ω R

120 µF C | 150 µF C

2ND-ORDER

TWO 15" WOOFERS IN ISOBARIC PUSH-PULL

SYSTEM 7

NOTES:
• = CONNECTIONS
µF = MICROFARADS
mH = MILLIHENRIES
Ω = OHMS

b. Crossover Network

c. System 7 Cabinet with Drivers Mounted

Figure 8-20. System 7 Driver Mounting, Grille Screens, and Crossover Network

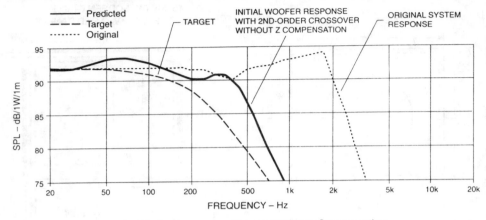

a. 2nd-Order Crossover without Impedance Compensation

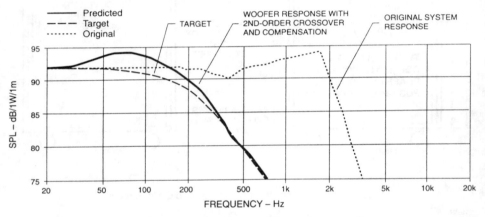

b. 2nd-Order Crossover with Impedance Compensation

Figure 8-21. System 7 Woofer Crossover Response with 2nd-Order Crossover

Follow the assembly steps for constructing System 7 as given in Figure 8-19. Start by constructing the 24" x 18" x 18" sealed boxes which house the isobaric, push-pull pairs of 15" woofers. The woofers mount in the top of each sealed box on opposite sides of a 6 15/16" hole cut in the top. Four panels—front, back, and two end panels—are fitted and fastened to the outside of the sealed boxes. In the two end panels (18" x 41"), there is a 14" diameter hole opening the chamber formed to the air. In the front panel (19 1/2" x 41"), there is a rectangular hole (10" x 13") on the upper right side and three vertical circular holes for a midrange, tweeter, and a midrange, respectively, on the upper left side as shown in *Figures 8-19a* and *8-20a*. An opening for the terminal plate needs to be cut in the back panel (19 1/2" x 41"). This can be done before or after attaching it to the sealed box. The top, also with a 14" diameter hole, finishes the top of the panels. Finish the openings in the top and end panels with a 15" grille screen. The rectangular opening

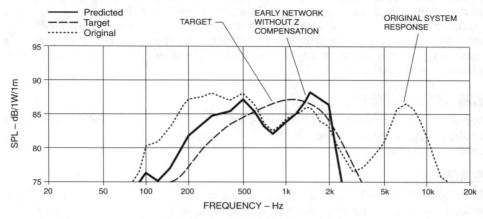

a. Early Crossover Midrange Response

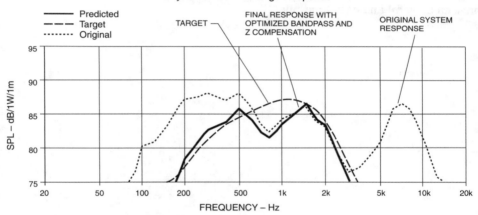

b. Final Optimized Crossover Response with Impedance Compensation

Figure 8-22. System 7 Midrange Crossover Response

in the front is covered by a grille frame which is built from 1″ × 3/4″ stock and covered with grille cloth. Since these cabinets will be quite heavy, screw four heavy duty casters onto the bottom of each cabinet. Use large plastic cups behind each of the 4″ midrange drivers to isolate the rear wave; each cup must be short enough to avoid the downward firing 15″ woofer. *Figure 8-20c* shows a cabinet assembled but without the top and grille screens and frame in place.

The 3-way crossover is an optimized design, crossed over at the rate of 12 dB/octave at 275 Hz and at the rate of 18 dB/octave at 2200 Hz. *Figure 8-21a* shows that using a 2nd-order crossover in the woofer section without impedance compensation overshoots the target curve considerably. Once impedance compensation is introduced, *Figure 8-21b* shows that the predicted response aligns with the target curve except for a slight increase between 50 Hz and 150 Hz. This increase may help compensate for diffraction losses likely to occur in this region. Shifted frequencies were used in the optimization of the bandpass section. *Figure 8-22a* shows the predicted midrange response at an early stage of crossover development. Once the bandpass section was optimized and impedance compensation was introduced, *Figure 8-22b* shows the response in close alignment with the target curve. Hopefully, a bandpass gain will boost the sagging natural response of the 4" paper cones which occurs between 500 and 1500 Hz.

FINISHING CABINETS

Speakers for Your Home and Automobile, a book also published by PROMPT Publications, is a good source for information and tips on how to finish any of the cabinets you build.

SUMMARY

This concludes the discussion of speaker systems whose designs are extended and refined by using more specific component data, more sophisticated calculations, available PC software, and unique designs. We hope that you find the information presented useful and easy to apply.

Appendix

Conversions

Prefixes for Powers of Ten

Engineers and technicians used a shorthand of prefixes so that large numbers of zeros before or after a number do not have to be carried along in a mathematical calculation. Here are what the prefixes mean:

Prefix	Symbol		Multiplication Factor
exa	E	10^{18} =	1,000,000,000,000,000,000
peta	P	10^{15} =	1,000,000,000,000,000
tera	T	10^{12} =	1,000,000,000,000
giga	G	10^{9} =	1,000,000,000
mega	M	10^{6} =	1,000,000
kilo	k	10^{3} =	1,000
hecto	h	10^{2} =	100
deca	da	10^{1} =	10
(unit)		10^{0} =	1
deci	d	10^{-1} =	0.1
centi	c	10^{-2} =	0.01
milli	m	10^{-3} =	0.001
micro	u	10^{-6} =	0.000001
nano	n	10^{-9} =	0.000000001
pico	p	10^{-12} =	0.000000000001
femto	f	10^{-15} =	0.000000000000001
atto	a	10^{-18} =	0.000000000000000001

Metric – Linear, Area and Volume Units

Metric to English	Multiply Metric Unit by
mm to inch *(linear)*	0.03937
cm to inch	0.3937
meter to foot	3.2808
cm^2 to $inches^2$ *(area)*	0.155
$meters^2$ to ft^2	10.763
$meters^3$ to ft^3 *(volume)*	35.314
liters to ft^3	0.0353

English to Metric	Multiply English Unit by
inch to mm *(linear)*	25.4
inch to cm	2.54
foot to meter	0.3048
$inches^2$ to cm^2 *(area)*	6.4516
ft^2 to $meters^2$	0.0929
ft^3 to $meters^3$ *(volume)*	0.02831
ft^3 to liters	28.32

Fractional Dimensions – English to Metric

Inches		Millimeters	Inches		Millimeters	Inches		Millimeters
$1/64$	0.016	0.397	$23/64$	0.359	9.128	$11/16$	0.688	17.463
$1/32$	0.031	0.794	$3/8$	0.375	9.525	$45/64$	0.703	17.859
$3/64$	0.047	1.191	$25/64$	0.391	9.922	$23/32$	0.719	18.256
$1/16$	0.063	1.588	$13/32$	0.406	10.319	$47/64$	0.734	18.653
$5/64$	0.078	1.984	$27/64$	0.422	10.716	$3/4$	0.750	19.050
$3/32$	0.094	2.381	$7/16$	0.438	11.113	$49/64$	0.766	19.447
$7/64$	0.109	2.778	$29/64$	0.453	11.509	$25/32$	0.781	19.844
$1/8$	0.125	3.175	$15/32$	0.469	11.906	$51/64$	0.797	20.241
$9/64$	0.141	3.572	$31/64$	0.484	12.303	$13/16$	0.813	20.638
$5/32$	0.156	3.969	$1/2$	0.500	12.700	$53/64$	0.828	21.034
$3/16$	0.188	4.762	$33/64$	0.516	13.097	$27/32$	0.844	21.431
$13/64$	0.203	5.159	$17/32$	0.531	13.494	$55/64$	0.859	21.828
$7/32$	0.219	5.556	$35/64$	0.547	13.891	$7/8$	0.875	22.225
$15/64$	0.234	5.953	$9/16$	0.563	14.288	$57/64$	0.891	22.622
$1/4$	0.250	6.350	$37/64$	0.578	14.684	$29/32$	0.906	23.019
$17/64$	0.266	6.747	$19/32$	0.594	15.081	$59/64$	0.922	23.416
$9/32$	0.281	7.144	$39/64$	0.609	15.478	$15/16$	0.938	23.813
$19/64$	0.297	7.541	$5/8$	0.625	15.875	$61/64$	0.953	24.209
$5/16$	0.313	7.938	$41/64$	0.641	16.272	$31/32$	0.969	24.606
$21/64$	0.328	8.334	$21/32$	0.656	16.669	1.0	1.000	25.400
$11/32$	0.344	8.731	$43/64$	0.672	17.066			

Powers of Ten

Powers of ten are used as shorthand for writing zeros before and/or after numbers; therefore, powers of ten become very convenient for the manipulation of mathematical calculations. For example:

For **Multiplication**, powers of ten add algebraically:

$E = IR = 3\ \mu A(3 \times 10^{-6}) \times 6\ M\Omega(6 \times 10^{+6}) = 18$ volts

$E = IR = 10\ mA(10 \times 10^{-3}) \times 100\ \Omega(1 \times 10^{+2}) = 10 \times 10^{-1}\ V = 1\ V$

For **Division**, powers of ten subtract algebraically:

$$I = \frac{E}{R} = \frac{100\ V}{20\ k\Omega} = \frac{1 \times 10^{+2}}{20 \times 10^{+3}} = \frac{1 \times 10^{+2}}{2 \times 10^{+4}} = \frac{1}{2} \times 10^{+2} \times 10^{-4} = 0.5 \times 10^{-2}$$
$$= 5 \times 10^{-3}$$
$$= 5\ mA$$

$$R = \frac{E}{I} = \frac{10\ V}{2\ \mu A} = \frac{1 \times 10^{+1}}{2 \times 10^{-6}} = 0.5 \times 10^{+1} \times 10^{+6} = 5 \times 10^{+6} = 5\ M\Omega$$

For **Addition and Subtraction** of numbers which powers of ten, both numbers must be expressed in the same power of ten:

$20\ mA + 20\ \mu A = 20 \times 10^{-3} + 20 \times 10^{-6} = 20 \times 10^{-3} + 0.02 \times 10^{-3} = 20.02\ mA$

$10\ V + 10\ mV = 10 + 10 \times 10^{-3} = 10 + 0.01 = 10.01\ V$

Sources for Products Not Readily Available in Electronics Parts Stores

Software

Speaker Enclosure Design
TOP BOX
ORCA Design
1531 Lookout Drive
Agoura, CA 91301
Telephone: (818) 707-1629

Crossover Design
PXO
Old Colony Sound Laboratory
P.O. Box 243
Peterborough, NH 03458-0243
Telephone: (603) 924-6526

Electronic Test Equipment

The Woofer Tester
C & S Audio Labs
P.O. Box 1012
Savage, MD 20763-1012

*Warble-Tone Generator
& Mitey Mike*
Old Colony Sound Laboratory
P.O Box 243
Peterborough, NH 03458-0243
Telephone: (603) 924-6526

Metal Chassis for Warble-Tone Generator
SESCOM
2100 Ward Drive
Henderson, NV 89015-4249
Telephone: (800) 634-3457

MLSSA
DRA Laboratories
607 W. Nettletree Rd.
Sterling, VA 22170
Telephone: (813) 927-2617

BK Model 3011B
Maxtec INT'L Group
6470 W. Cortland St.
Chicago, IL 60635

Cabinets

Zalytron Industries Crop.
469 Jericho Turnpike
Mineola, NY 11501
Telephone: (516) 747-3515

Virgin Cabinets
R.R. #1
Desbarats, Ontario, Canada
POR 1EQ
Telephone: (705) 736-2826

Crossover Components

Meniscus Audio Group
2575 28th Street S.W., Unit 2
Wyoming, MI 49509-2105
Telephone: (616) 534-9121

Madisound Speaker Components
8608 University Green
P.O. Box 44283
Madison, WI 53744-4283
Telephone: (608) 831-3433

Crossover Optimization Programs

LMP

Although not a full optimization program, LMP can take into account diffraction loss, phase shifts due to time delays, driver sensitivity and the driver fall-off rate/crossover order interaction. Available from: Old Colony Sound Laboratory, P.O. Box 243, Peterborough, NH 03458-0243, (603) 924-6526.

CALSOD

CALSOD is *not* an easy program to understand, but it can alter the values of the crossover components until a curve is produced that most closely matches an ideal "target" curve. To use CALSOD, you must print out a 243-page manual from the program. Available from: Old Colony Sound Laboratory, P.O. Box 243, Peterborough, N.H. 03458-0243, (603) 924-6526.

LEAP

An expensive program that is a current favorite among many speaker design professionals. A separate program, called LMS, can measure frequency response, impedance and Thiele-Small parameters. Comes with two 500-page manuals. An IBM demonstration disc and further information are available from: LinearX Systems, 7556 S.W. Bridgeport Rd., Portland OR 97224.

AC Circuits and Amplifier Power Output

AC Circuits

An alternating-current circuit is one in which the current periodically changes in magnitude and direction as shown in *Figure A.* The sine-wave alternating-current voltage varies in magnitude periodically with time as shown in *Figure Aa.* It is supplying current to a driver. During the positive alteration of *Figure Ab,* the direction of current is clockwise, and the driver cone moves forward. During the negative alternation of *Figure Ac,* the direction of current is counterclockwise, and the driver cone moves backward. The movement of the driver cone is proportional to the magnitude of the current.

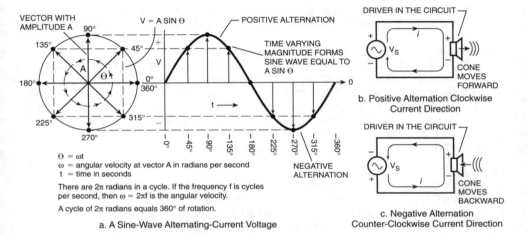

$$\Theta = \omega t$$
ω = angular velocity at vector A in radians per second
t = time in seconds

There are 2π radians in a cycle. If the frequency f is cycles per second, then $\omega = 2\pi f$ is the angular velocity.

A cycle of 2π radians equals 360° of rotation.

a. A Sine-Wave Alternating-Current Voltage

b. Positive Alternation Clockwise Current Direction

c. Negative Alternation Counter-Clockwise Current Direction

Figure A. A Sine-Wave Alternating-Current Voltage Producing Current in a Driver Circuit

Amplifier Power

Power is the time rate of doing work. In an ac resistive circuit, the power delivered or dissipated in a component is equal to V_{rms} across the component times the I_{rms} through the component expressed in watts. One volt times one ampere equals one watt. If the voltage output from an amplifier is 20 V_{rms}, and the driver's rated impedance is 4 ohms, then, by Ohm's law, the current, I_{rms}, in the voice coil is 5 A. The power delivered to the driver is 20 × 5 = 100 watts.

A common question is "Can I get more power output from my amplifier by paralleling speaker systems across each channel output?" The table shows the comparison. First, for a single speaker system connected across each channel, second, for two 8-ohm speaker systems connected in parallel across each channel, and third, for three 8-ohm speaker systems connected in parallel across each channel. The amplifier output is assumed to be constant at 20 V_{rms}.

With one 8-ohm speaker, the amplifier current is 2.5 A and the power to each speaker system is 50 watts (P = 20V × 2.5A). Connecting two 8-ohm speaker systems in parallel results in a total impedance of 4 ohms, an amplifier current of 5 A and a total power output of 100 watts (20 V × 5A). *The amplifier must now deliver twice the current.*

Three 8-ohm speakers in parallel results in a load on the amplifier of 2.7 ohms (R = 8/3), an amplifier current of 7.4 A, a total power output of 148 watts (20V × 7.4 A), and a power output per speaker system of 49.3 watts. The amplifier current is now almost three times the current for the 8-ohm load. A 4-ohm load can be handled by almost any modern amplifier; however, unless the amplifier is expressly designed for the purpose, trying to use the 2.7-ohm system can be bad news and place too much current demand on most amplifiers. What is of particular concern are the solid-state devices inside the amplifier. Since the output voltage is constant at 20 volts, the devices must dissipate 150 watts at the highest current. As they increase in temperature, their leakage current increases and their breakdown voltage decreases—a disastrous condition that can lead to runaway and permanent damage.

Power Output and Amplifier Current for Various Speaker System

Driver In Parallel	Resultant Load (Ω)	Amplifier Current (A)	Total Power (W)	Power per Spkr (W)
One 8 Ω	8	2.5	50	50
Two 8 Ω	4	5.0	100	50
Three 8 Ω	2.7	7.4	148	49.3

Books and Articles for Reference and Further Detail

Three books, ranging from basic to advanced, may be of help to you in speaker building:
1. *Speakers for Your Home and Automobile*, by Gordon McComb, Alvis Evans and Eric Evans. Published by PROMPT Publications, Division Howard W. Sams & Company.
2. *Designing, Building and Testing Your Own Speaker System*, 3rd Edition, by David Weems. Published by Tab Books, Division McGraw-Hill, Inc.
3. *The Loudspeaker Design Cookbook*, 4th edition, by Vance Dickason, Published by Audio Amateur Press. Available from Old Colony Sound Laboratories, Ibid.

Two periodicals can help you to develop a creative outlook on speaker building:
1. *Audio Talk*, published by the Polydax Speaker Corporation. Free on request; write to: Polydax Co., 10 Upton Drive, Wilmington, MA 01887.
2. *Speaker Builder*, published by Audio Amateur Press. Available by subscription: PO Box 494, Peterborough, NH, 03458-0494, Telephone: (800) 524-9464. Back issues are available from Speaker Builder. Listed below are several important articles from Speaker Builder that can be considered essential reading for a deeper understanding of the following subjects:

Crossovers
- *Passive Crossover Networks—Part I*, by Robert Bullock, III, Issue 1/1985.
- *Passive Crossover Networks—Part II*, by Robert Bullock, III, Issue 2/1985.
- *Passive Crossover Networks—Part V*, Robert Bullock, III, Issue 4/1987.
- *Real World Two-Way Crossovers*, by Ralph Gonzalez, Issue 1/1992.
- *Impedance Compensating Crossover*, by Max Knittel, Issue 1/1983.
- *Notch Filters*, by David Weems, Issue 1/1986.

The 3/2 Geometry and Multiple Drivers
- *A High Powered Satellite Speaker*, by Joseph D'Appolito, Issue 4/1984.

Vented Loudspeakers
- *Thiele, Small and Vented Loudspeaker Design—Part I*, by Robert Bullock III, Issue 4/1980.
- *Thiele, Small and Vented Loudspeaker Design—Part III*, by Robert Bullock III, Issue 2/1981.

Loudspeaker Measurement
- *How You Can Determine Design Parameters for Your Loudspeaker*, by Robert Bullock III, Issue 1/1981.

Closed Box Speakers
- *Trade-offs in Closed Box Alignment*, by G.R. Koonce, Issue 2/1984.

Bandpass Subwoofers
- *The Third Dimension: Symmetrically Loaded*, by Jean Magerand, Issue 6/1988.

Alternate Loudspeaker Enclosures
- *Transmission Line Loudspeakers*, by Gary Galo, Issue 1/1982.
- *The Tractix Horn Contour*, by Bruce Edgar, Issue 1/1981.

Glossary

acoustic feedback: A squealing sound when the output of an audio circuit is fed back in phase into the circuit's input.

acoustic fiberglass: Thin fiberglass material used as damping material inside speaker enclosures.

acoustic suspension: A speaker designed for, or used in, a sealed enclosure.

ac coupling: Coupling between electronic circuits that passes only alternating current and time varying signals, not direct current.

acoustics: The science or study of sound.

air suspension: An acoustic suspension speaker.

alternating current (ac): An electrical current that periodically changes in magnitude and direction.

ampere (A): The unit of measurement for electrical current in coulombs (6.25×10^{18} electrons) per second. There is one ampere in a circuit that has one ohm resistance when one volt is applied to the circuit. See Ohm's law.

amplifier: An electrical circuit designed to increase the current, voltage, or power of an applied signal.

amplitude: The relative strength (usually voltage) of a signal. Amplitude can be expressed as either a negative or positive number, depending on the signals being compared.

attenuation: The reduction, typically by some controlled amount, of an electrical signal.

audio frequency: The acoustic spectrum of human hearing, generally regarded to be between 20 Hz and 20,000 Hz.

baffle: A piece of wood inside an enclosure used to direct or block the movement of sound.

balance: Equal signal strength provided to both left and right stereo channels.

bandpass filter: An electric circuit designed to pass only middle frequencies. See also high-pass filter and low-pass filter.

basket: The metal frame of a speaker.

bass: The low end of the audio frequency spectrum: approximately 20 Hz to about 1000 Hz.

bass reflex: A ported reflex speaker enclosure.

battens: Small strips of wood placed inside a speaker system enclosure to reinforce its mating corners or to provide a mounting surface for front and back panels.

capacitor (C): A device made up of two metallic plates separated by a dielectric (insulating material). Used to store electrical energy in the electrostatic field between the plates. It produces an impedance to an ac current.

channel: The left or right signals of a stereo audio system.

circuit: A complete path that allows electrical current from one terminal of a voltage source to the other terminal.

clipping: A distortion caused by cutting off the peaks of audio signals. Clipping usually occurs in the amplifier when its input signal is too high or when the volume control is turned up too high.

coaxial driver: A speaker that is composed of two individual voice coils and cones; used for reproduction of sounds in two segments of the sound spectrum. See also triaxial driver.

coloration: "Smearing" sounds by adding frequencies due to intermodulation distortion. More prevalent at high audio frequencies.

compliance: The relative stiffness of a speaker suspension, typically indicated simply as "high" or "low," but technically specified as Vas.

cone: The cone-shaped diaphragm of a speaker attached to the voice coil. It produces pulsations of air that the ear detects as sound.

crossover network: An electric circuit or network that splits the audio frequencies into different bands for application to individual speakers.

current (I): The flow of charge measured in amperes.

damping: The reduction of movement of a speaker cone, due either to the electromechanical characteristics of the speaker driver and suspension, or the effects of frictional losses inside a speaker enclosure.

decibel (dB): A logarithmic scale used to denote a change in the relative strength of an electric signal or acoustic wave. It is a standard unit for expressing the ratio between power level P_1 and power level P_2. $dB = 10 \log_{10} P_1/P_2$. An increase of 3 dB is a doubling of electrical (or signal) power; an increase of 10 dB is a doubling of perceived loudness. The decibel is not an absolute measurement, actually, but indicates the relationship or ratio between two signal levels.

dielectric: The nonconducting material used to separate the plates of a capacitor or the conductors in transmission lines, or for insulating electrical contracts.

direct current (dc): Current in only one direction.

dispersion: The spreading of sound waves as they leave a speaker.

distortion: Any undesirable change in the characteristics of an audio signal.

dome tweeter: A high frequency speaker with a dome-shaped diaphragm that provides much better dispersion of high frequencies than standard cone speakers.

driver: The electromagnetic components of a speaker, typically consisting of a magnet and voice coil.

ducted port: A ported reflex speaker enclosure.

dynamic-range: The range of sound levels which a system can reproduce without distortion.

dynamic range: The range of sounds, expressed in decibels, between the softest and loudest portions.

equalizer: An adjustable audio filter inserted in a circuit to divide and adjust its frequency response.

equalization: As used in audio, the adjustment of frequency response to tailor the sound to match personal preferences, room acoustics, and speaker enclosure design.

farad: The basic unit of capacitance. A capacitor has a value of one farad when it can store one coulomb of charge with one volt across it.

filter: An electrical circuit designed to prevent or reduce the passage of certain frequencies.

flat response: The faithful reproduction of an audio signal; specifically, variations in output level of less than one decibel above or below a median level over the audio spectrum.

former: A paper, plastic, or metal cylinder around which is wound the wire that forms a speaker's voice coil. The former is mechanically connected to the speaker cone.

free air resonance: The natural resonant frequency of a woofer speaker when operating outside an enclosure.

frequency: The number of waves (or cycles) arriving at or passing a point in one second; expressed in hertz (or Hz).

frequency response: The range of frequencies that are faithfully reproduced by a given speaker or audio system.

fundamental or fundamental tone: The tone produced by the lowest frequency component of an audio signal.

full-range: A speaker designed to reproduce all or most of the sound spectrum.

golden ratio: The ratio of the depth, width, and height of a speaker enclosure, based on the Greek Golden Rectangle, and which most often provides the best sound. W = 1.0, Depth = 0.618W, Height = 1.618W

grille cloth: Fabric used to cover the speaker mounted in an enclosure.

ground: Refers to a point of (usually) zero voltage, and can pertain to a power circuit or a signal circuit.

harmonic: The multiple frequencies of a given sound, created by the interaction of signal waveforms. A "middle C" on the piano has a fundamental audio frequency of 256 Hz, but also a number of secondary higher frequencies (harmonics) that are odd and even multiples of this fundamental.

harmonic distortion: Harmonics artificially added by an electrical circuit or speaker, and are generally undesirable. It is expressed as a percentage of the original signal.

hertz: A unit of frequency equal to one cycle per second, named after German physicist H.R. Hertz.

high-fidelity: Commonly called hi-fi, it refers to the reproduction of sound with little or no distortion.

high-pass filter: An electric circuit designed to pass only high frequencies. See also bandpass filter and low-pass filter.

hiss: Audio noise that sounds like air escaping from a tire.

horn: A speaker design using its own funnel-shaped conduit to amplify, disperse, or modify the sounds generated by the internal diaphragm of the speaker.

hum: Audio noise that has a steady low frequency pitch, typically caused by the effects of induction by nearby ac lines or leakage of ac line frequency into an amplifier's signal circuits.

impedance: The opposition of a circuit or speaker to an alternating current.

inductance (L): The capability of a coil to store energy in a magnetic field surrounding it. It produces an impedance to an ac current.

L-pad: A type of potentiometer that maintains constant impedance at its input while varying the signal level at its output. L-pads are most often used as an external balance control or variable attenuator (volume control).

logarithm (log): The exponent to which a base number must be raised to obtain the original number.

low-pass filter: An electric circuit designed to pass only low frequencies. See also bandpass filter and high-pass filter.

midrange: A speaker designed to reproduce the middle frequencies of the sound spectrum, generally most efficient between about 1000 Hz to 4000 Hz.

mounting flange: The outer edges of a speaker frame which has pre-drilled holes to accept screws or bolts for securing it to the enclosure.

noise: An unwanted sound.

ohm (Ω): A unit of electrical resistance or impedance.

Ohm's law: A basic law of electric circuits. It states that the current I in amperes in a circuit is equal to the voltage E in volts divided by the resistance R in Ohms; thus, $I = E/R$.

passive radiator (or drone): A speaker with a cone but no driver components. The cone vibrates with the change in pressure inside the speaker enclosure. Typically used to increase bass output with no increase in electrical power. Acts in same manner as a port.

peak: The maximum amplitude of a voltage or current.

piezoelectric: A characteristic of some materials, especially crystal, that when subjected to electric voltage the material vibrates. Sometimes used in tweeters in place of a magnet, voice coil, and cone.

polarity: The orientation of magnetic or electric fields. The polarity of the incoming audio signal determines the direction of movement of the speaker cone.

ported reflex: A type of speaker enclosure that uses a duct or port to improve efficiency at low frequencies.

power: The time rate of doing work or the rate at which energy is used. A watt of electrical power is the use of one joule of energy per second. Watts of electrical power equals volts times amperes.

resonance: The tendency of a speaker to vibrate most at a particular frequency; sometimes referred to as natural frequency.

resistance: In electrical or electronic circuits, a characteristic of a material that opposes the flow of electrons. It results in loss of energy in a circuit dissipated as heat. Speakers have resistance that opposes current.

RMS: An acronym for root mean square. The RMS value of an alternating current produces the same heating effect in a circuit as the same value of a direct current.

signal: The desired portion of electrical information.

signal-to-noise (S/N): The ratio, expressed in dB, between the signal (sound you want) and noise (sound you don't want).

sine wave: The waveform of a pure alternating current or voltage. It deviates about a zero point to a positive value and a negative value. Audio signals are sine waves or combinations of sine waves.

sound pressure level (SPL): The loudness of an acoustic wave stated in dB that is proportional to the logarithm of its intensity.

spider: The flexible material that supports the former, voice coil, and inside portion of the cone within the speaker frame.

surround: The outer suspension of a speaker cone; the surround connects the outside portion of the cone to the speaker frame.

suspension: See surround.

three-way: A type of speaker system composed of three ranges of speakers, specifi-cally a tweeter, midrange, and woofer. See also two-way.

total harmonic distortion (THD): The percentage, in relation to a pure input signal, of harmonically derived frequencies introduced in the sound reproducing circuitry and hi-fi equipment (including the speakers).

treble: The upper end of the audio spectrum, usually reproduced by a tweeter.

transient response: The instantaneous change in an electronic circuit's output response when input circuit conditions suddenly change from one steady-state condition to another.

triaxial driver: A speaker that is composed of three individual voice coils and cones; used for the reproduction of sounds in three segments of the sound spectrum. See also coaxial driver.

tweeter: A speaker designed to reproduce the high or treble range of the sound spectrum, generally most efficient from about 4000 Hz to 20,000 Hz.

two-way: A type of speaker system composed of two ranges of speakers, consisting of any two of the following: a tweeter, midrange, and woofer. See also three-way. Some midrange speakers are classified as midrange/tweeter.

voice coil: The wire wound around the speaker former. The former is mechanically connected to the speaker cone and causes the cone to vibrate in response to the audio current in the voice coil.

warble: Producing musical sounds that cover a wide audio frequency spectrum with melodious runs, trills, quavers, and many turns and variations.

watt: A unit of electrical power.

whizzer: A small supplementary cone attached to the center of the speaker's main cone for the purpose of increasing high frequency response.

woofer: A speaker designed to reproduce the low frequencies of the sound spectrum, generally most efficient from about 20 Hz to 1000 Hz.

Index

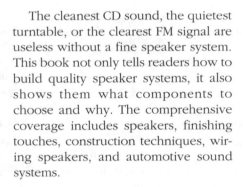

Semiconductor Cross Reference Book Fourth Edition

Howard W. Sams & Company

This newly revised and updated reference book is the most comprehensive guide to replacement data available for engineers, technicians, and those who work with semiconductors. With more than 490,000 part numbers, type numbers, and other identifying numbers listed, technicians will have no problem locating the replacement or substitution information needed. There is not another book on the market that can rival the breadth and reliability of information available in the fourth edition of the *Semiconductor Cross Reference Book*.

IC Cross Reference Book Second Edition

Howard W. Sams & Company

The engineering staff of Howard W. Sams & Company assembled the *IC Cross Reference Book* to help readers find replacements or substitutions for more than 35,000 ICs and modules. It is an easy-to-use cross reference guide and includes part numbers for the United States, Europe, and the Far East. This reference book was compiled from manufacturers' data and from the analysis of consumer electronics devices for PHOTOFACT® service data, which has been relied upon since 1946 by service technicians worldwide.

Professional Reference
688 pages ◆ Paperback ◆
8-1/2 x 11"
ISBN: 0-7906-1080-9 ◆ Sams: 61080
$24.95 ($33.95 Canada) ◆ August 1996

Professional Reference
192 pages ◆ Paperback ◆
8-1/2 x 11"
ISBN: 0-7906-1096-5 ◆ Sams: 61096
$19.95 ($26.99 Canada) ◆ November 1996

**CALL 1-800-428-7267 TODAY FOR THE NAME OF
YOUR NEAREST PROMPT PUBLICATIONS DISTRIBUTOR**

The Video Book
Gordon McComb

TV Video Systems
L.W. Pena & Brent A. Pena

Televisions and video cassette recorders have become part of everyday life, but few people know how to get the most out of these home entertainment devices. *The Video Book* offers easy-to-read text and clearly illustrated examples to guide readers through the use, installation, connection, and care of video system components. Simple enough for the new buyer, yet detailed enough to assure proper connection of the units after purchase, this book is a necessary addition to the library of every modern video consumer.

Knowing which video programming source to choose, and knowing what to do with it once you have it, can seem overwhelming. Covering standard hard-wired cable, large-dish satellite systems, and DSS, *TV Video Systems* explains the different systems, how they are installed, their advantages and disadvantages, and how to troubleshoot problems. This book presents easy-to-understand information and illustrations covering installation instructions, home options, apartment options, detecting and repairing problems, and more. The in-depth chapters guide you through your TV video project to a successful conclusion.

Video Technology
192 pages ✦ Paperback ✦ 6 x 9"
ISBN: 0-7906-1030-2 ✦ Sams:
61030
$16.95 ($22.99 Canada) ✦ October 1992

Video Technology
124 pages ✦ Paperback ✦ 6 x 9"
ISBN: 0-7906-1082-5 ✦ Sams:
61082
$14.95 ($20.95 Canada) ✦ June 1996

Dear Reader: *We'd like your views on the books we publish.*

PROMPT® Publications, a division of Howard W. Sams & Company (A Bell Atlantic Company), is dedicated to bringing you timely and authoritative documentation and information you can use. You can help us in our continuing effort to meet your information needs. Please take a few moments to answer the questions below. Your answers will help us serve you better in the future.

1. What is the title of the book you purchased?_____
2. Where do you usually buy books?_____
3. Where did you buy this book?_____
4. What did you like most about the book?_____
5. What did you like least?_____
6. Is there any other information you'd like included?_____
7. In what subject areas would you like us to publish more books? (Please check the boxes next to your fields of interest.)

❑ Audio Equipment Repair   ❑ Home Appliance Repair

❑ Camcorder Repair   ❑ Mobile Communications

❑ Computer Repair   ❑ Security Systems

❑ Electronic Concepts Theory   ❑ Sound System Installation

❑ Electronic Projects/Hobbies   ❑ TV Repair

❑ Electronic Reference   ❑ VCR Repair

8. Are there other subjects that you'd like to see books about? _____
_____
9. Comments _____
_____
_____

• •

Name _____
Address _____
City _____ State/ZIP _____
E-Mail _____

Would you like a *FREE* PROMPT® Publications catalog? ❑Yes ❑ No

Thank you for helping us make our books better for all of our readers. Please drop this postage-paid card into the nearest mailbox.

For more information about PROMPT® Publications, see your authorized Howard Sams distributor or call 1-800-428-7267 for the name of your nearest PROMPT® Publications distributor.

PROMPT.
PUBLICATIONS

A Division of *Howard W. Sams & Company*
A Bell Atlantic Company
2647 Waterfront Parkway, East Dr.
Indianapolis, IN 46214-2041

BUSINESS REPLY MAIL

FIRST-CLASS MAIL   PERMIT NO. 1317   INDIANAPOLIS IN

POSTAGE WILL BE PAID BY ADDRESSEE

PROMPT
P U B L I C A T I O N S

A DIVISION OF HOWARD W SAMS & CO
2647 WATERFRONT PARKWAY EAST DRIVE
INDIANAPOLIS IN 46209-1418

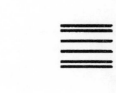

NO POSTAGE
NECESSARY
IF MAILED
IN THE
UNITED STATES